DANA HOUSE
FRANK LLOYD WRIGHT

DANA HOUSE
FRANK LLOYD WRIGHT

THOMAS A HEINZ

ACADEMY EDITIONS

ACKNOWLEDGEMENTS

I would firstly like to thank Al Drap and Rich Branom, who made it possible for me to visit the Dana House in 1972 for the first time, and to Payne Thomas and Mr W N Lyon, who granted many requests over the next ten years from the three of us. Rich would often play the grand piano in the Gallery while Al and I photographed and explored the mysterious nooks and crannies, trying at first to comprehend the house and later to reassemble it visually and textually from our slides and memories. I am very grateful to Al and Rich for these valuable opportunities. Rich has also been helpful in additional research and in reviewing parts of the text. As a result of these many visits, I was able to measure the furniture and assemble over two thousand photographs of the Dana House before the work on the restoration.

Cynthia Durko helped in the first of the precision photo sessions and in getting images for the State of Illinois. Heidi Hombs Cortelyn and George Dark struggled with my equipment the one time I brought accessory lighting into the house.

Scott Thomas, a successful Chicago editor and former Thomas Publishing employee, helped me to access information and uncover many facts and details, often those that were important but could easily have been missed.

Penny Severens showed an enthusiastic interest in the house as expressed in a steady stream of articles she sent me from Springfield newspapers.

Donald Hallmark's interest in the Dana House was a result of his Doctoral study on Richard W Bock, the sculptor. Dr Hallmark consequently brought this collection to Greenville College, located between Springfield and St Louis. He has shown continuous and enthusiastic endurance, even after having been the State's Site Superintendent for nearly fifteen years.

Donald Hoffman's precise work ensured that details were not overlooked throughout his studies and analysis of other buildings and insights into Wright's inspirations.

Walter Creese and John Replinger were my professors at the University of Illinois. They introduced me to the legacy of Walter Burley Griffin and William Drummond, graduates of the university. I would like to thank them for supporting the research into Griffin and Wright that Al Drap and I pursued.

Henry-Russell Hitchcock inspired me greatly with his rigorous inquisitiveness into my work. I often felt perforated after even a short session with him, but he only sought the best analysis.

Edgar Kaufmann, Jr, had his first Big Mac at the Dana House dining table. He was somewhat overwhelmed at the fine state of preservation as well as the quality and quantity of the furnishings. The Dana House helped him understand Wright's use of oak.

Bruce Pfeiffer, Penny Fowler, and the late Wes Peters of The Frank Lloyd Wright Foundation were very helpful with information and insights.

Thanks to Carol Trone, a quiet supporter of all interested in knowing more about the Dana House, through its Sumac Bookshop. Cathy Liesman is a State employee (on site now) who cares for the house but also understands it in a way that few others ever will. Her description of the light at dawn striking the fountain doors is breathtaking. David Diedrich was generous with his information and took the time to discuss minute details regarding Susan and her house.

My thanks also to Ann Terando who assisted in the final draft.

I learned much from Wayne Andrews and Maynard Parker's photos, though none are used here.

Finally, my thanks to John Stoddart (Managing Director), Maggie Toy (Managing Editor), Andrea Bettella (Art Editor), Mario Bettella (Chief Designer), Ramona Khambatta (Editorial) and David Breen (Design) at Academy Editions in London.

All figures in brackets refer to the official opus numbers of The Frank Lloyd Wright Archives at The Frank Lloyd Wright Foundation, Taliesin West.

Page 2: Flower in the Crannied Wall sculpture

First published in Great Britain in 1995 by
ACADEMY EDITIONS
an imprint of
ACADEMY GROUP LTD
42 Leinster Gardens, London W2 3AN
Member of the VCH Publishing Group

ISBN: 1 85490 442 1

Distributed in the United States of America by
ST MARTIN'S PRESS, 175 FIFTH AVENUE, NEW YORK, NY 10010

Printed and bound in Singapore

CONTENTS

INTRODUCTION

The Dana House (9905) was built almost as a memorial to Susan's father, Rheuna Lawrence. It now stands as reminder of the ability of a client and an architect to produce a uniquely beautiful work of art – one that can even be left out in the rain!

There is much mystery surrounding the house. There might be less mystery if the design of the house was more conventional, but unusual features beg an explanation. There is little in the form of material evidence from either Susan Dana or Wright regarding the building and early occupancy of the house, which is not only unusual, but frustrating too, as even a small number of documents, letters and photographs would help reveal true reasons and meanings, hence laying speculation to rest.

The mystery stems from Susan Dana, who, as a wealthy, fatherless, childless widow, hired an ambitious young architect who upset convention with his all-embracing artistic designs, to build her house. Taking what was considered his rather eccentric style into account, it initially seems strange that the Dana House was designed to embrace an existing, older and more conventional building, instead of being built new on a large estate on the edge of town. With the custom art glass, a unique sculpture which can be seen through the glass front door and the startlingly straightforward brown custom furniture, the interior of the house was as much a complete reversal of the popular Victorian taste as the exterior. At the turn of the century, in an area which strictly maintained custom and tradition, Susan's decision to commission Wright, and her unerring commitment to his beliefs can only be seen as courageous.

At the end of the century, nearly one hundred years later, the Dana House is a national treasure for us to behold. No individual photograph or collection of photographs could truly convey how beautiful and complex the building is. This one building houses the best of Wright's furniture, murals, art glass and sculpture, and to see it firsthand is the only way it can be truly appreciated as a whole. The house is now open to the public and so is easily accessible.

The odds that this work of art would come down to us through the years, nearly complete and nearly in its original state, is as remarkable as the craftsmanship of the house and the interior itself. The Dana House is home to the largest collection of Wright's designs with the most art glass and free-standing furniture of all his buildings. The majority of Wright's houses have little of their original furnishings left, but this is fortunately not the case with the Dana House. Not only is this pleasing but it is historically very important as well, enabling us to understand Wright's intentions. However, the harmony of detail and colour, light and proportions, landscaping and texture is so delicate that a true and full appreciation of Wright's genius is yet to occur.

Newly discovered buildings, projects and drawings, as well as lost windows and furniture are frequently found, but without a complete and comprehensive documented account, it is difficult to assess his long and prolific career. Our study and understanding of how his buildings functioned and how best to preserve them has only just begun. The exposure of the Dana House and its treasures will accelerate our understanding of the work of a genius who changed the course of architectural history.

Susan Lawrence Dana House, old photograph
This rare old photograph is from a book of house portraits of Springfield which also showed many of the neighbouring mansions on what was known as Aristocracy Hill. The name is curious because there are no real hills in or around Springfield. One is quite struck by the flatness of the prairie. *Photo courtesy of Rich Branom.*

SUSAN LAWRENCE DANA'S BACKGROUND

The focus of much work on the life of Susan Lawrence has concentrated upon the tragic deaths of her children, husbands and parents. In actual fact, Susan Lawrence was married for an aggregate of thirty-three years. In 1883, at the age of twenty-one, she married Edwin Whitney Dana who died prematurely in an Oregon mining accident when Susan was thirty-seven. Her second husband was born in 1887, a year after the birth of her first child. The child died the same day it was born and her second child, born in 1887, lived for only two months.

Susan married Jorgen Constantin Dahl, twenty-four years her junior, twelve years after the death of her first husband. Susan was forty-nine and Jorgen, twenty-five. Dahl died prematurely as well, fifteen months later of acute Bright's Disease (a kidney disease) in Chicago. She married for the third and final time at the age of fifty-two. Charles A Gehrmann was a grade school classmate of Susan's, and like her first husband, came from a mining background. They were married in Oakland, California in 1915. He moved to Texas on his own in 1920 and divorced Susan in 1930, two years after she moved out of the Dana House and into the White Cottage.

Susan's father, Rheuna Drake Lawrence was born in Cedarville, Ohio in 1837, and in 1859 married seventeen year old Mary Agnes Maxey in Springfield. He was quite an entrepreneur, having been a mason, merchant and a supplier of wood cracker boxes and railroad ties for the Union Army in the Civil War. In 1871, Mr Lawrence helped expand the railroad into Missouri and Illinois. Since coal was plentiful in central Illinois and the railroads needed a commodity to ship, it was natural that he ventured into the coal mining business in Springfield's Sangamon County in 1872, and in silver and gold mines in Colorado and Oregon by the 1880s. In 1901, at the age of sixty-four, he died leaving an estate estimated to be worth over $3,000,000.

Mr Lawrence was a civic-minded businessman. He had been a board member and president of the Board of Education for over eight years and a school, constructed by the Springfield Board of Education was named after him in 1903. It was designed by George Helme, a local Springfield architect. Susan was interested in having a Lawrence Memorial Library of Wright's design included in the school to commemorate her father and celebrate their common interest in education. An original drawing of the room is housed at the Archives of The Frank Lloyd Wright Foundation in Arizona. The Memorial Library was thought to be a part of the Dana House for many years since Susan loaned books to the local children from her own home. It was not until recently that volunteers at the Dana-Thomas House explored and found the Lawrence Memorial Library at the school. The school is located several blocks to the southwest of the Dana House and the Memorial Library Room has been rebuilt according to the original plans and photographs.

Mrs Rheuna Lawrence lived and travelled with Susan before and after Rheuna's death. She died of cardial asthma in Savannah, Georgia, just after the Dana House was finished in 1905 at the age of 64, on the return leg of a trip from Florida and the Bahamas. Her funeral was held in the Dana House.

While much is known about Susan's life, there is little known about her education. She was born on October 13, 1862 in

Susan's mother and father

LEFT TO RIGHT: Mary Agnes Maxey Lawrence, born 1841, Springfield, Illinois; Rheuna Drake Lawrence, born 1837, Cedarville, Ohio. They were married on January 24, 1859.

DH 89.F.0.3 & 0.1 from the Archives of the Dana-Thomas House, State Historic Site.

Springfield, the only child of Rheuna and Mary Lawrence, and attended the Betty Stewart School in Springfield – a private school which included both grammar and high schools. There are no records of how long she attended the school, nor of any particular subjects in which she might have had an interest. She had many of her own books, believed enough in education to fund a library in honour of her father, and had a regular lending library in her own house. Susan also supported the efforts of Wright's aunts at Hillside Home School (8703).

Because of her wealth, Susan was able to indulge most of her interests in clothing, entertaining and a great variety of intellectual pursuits. The local newspaper had several mentions by Wright about her art collection, yet early photographs of the house show no evidence of this. There are mostly Wright-designed pieces or those that would be compatible or recommended by Wright, such as Teco pottery and ferns. Several examples of Wright's metal work are shown, such as the copper urns and weedholders. Only one piece of art hangs on any wall that can be seen, just outside her mother's bedroom. The subject and artist are not identifiable. Most walls, as was and is typical in Wright interiors, are bare.

Susan must have had a passion for photography, as the first scheme shows a large darkroom in the basement of the gallery and the second scheme relocates it behind the fireplace masonry to the west. However, none of Susan's photographs have been identified. It would be very revealing to locate one of her photo albums of the house.

Susan travelled widely at a time of great expansion and exploration throughout the world and experienced the industrial revolution firsthand. The telephone, television, automobiles, airplanes and atom bombs were all invented during her lifetime. Many of these inventions influenced the house she built with Wright. For example, hers was one of the first houses to fully incorporate electricity in Springfield.

One of the many mysteries is how Susan Lawrence Dana and Frank Lloyd Wright became acquainted. There is some suggestion on the part of the Site Superintendent, Dr Donald Hallmark, that Susan may have met Wright's Aunt Jennie in Minneapolis when she and her husband, Edwin Dana, resided there in the mid-1880s. Jane Lloyd Jones (often called Jennie) was the director of kindergarten training schools in St Paul, and in Wright's autobiography it is noted that Susan Lawrence Dana donated $27,000 to construct the science wing of the Hillside Home School in Spring Green in 1902: 'I had found money for them [Aunt Nell and Jane] when the 1902 buildings were built. One of my clients, Mrs Susan Lawrence Dana, gave them the little Art and Science buildings, the next School building and full equipment. Complete. She loaned the Aunts twenty-seven thousand dollars more to help complete the main School building'. Susan, along with Oak Park's C E Roberts, was a shareholder in the school's corporation and continued to be through the teens. It is not known if Susan met Wright's aunts before or after she met Wright. Mr and Mrs Dana moved to Minneapolis in 1883, after their wedding. They then moved to Chicago in 1888, and by 1893 they had returned to Springfield. Four years later they moved to Oregon to oversee one of Rheuna Lawrence's mines.

A second opportunity for Wright and Susan to meet, noted by Dr Hallmark, may have been at the initial meeting of the new Daughters of the American Revolution Chapter on January 24, 1896, in Oak Park. This meeting may have been attended by Wright's wife, Catherine Tobin Wright and mother, Anna Lloyd Wright, both of whom were founding members of Oak Park's George Rogers Clark Chapter.

On the site of Rheuna Lawrence's house, Wright built his Prairie style house, wrapping it around the earlier house. In Wright's autobiography, his recollection was, 'the Dana House in Springfield – dear old Mother Lawrence, salt risen bread, blackberry preserves and the way we kept faith with the old homestead'. The reference to the 'old homestead' may give a clue about how Susan felt about the Lawrence House and why she required it was to be kept as part of the work undertaken.

The years 1905 to 1912 were the peak years of entertaining at the Dana House. She was close to the Governor and Mrs Charles Deneen. A particular reception for over one thousand people was held on June 22, 1906 and the house was designed with large social events such as this in mind.

Susan's interests in the Springfield social scene were slowly displaced by her interests in spirituality and mysticism. These interests were developing in 1905 when she tried to contact her parents through spiritualists and slate writing. Spiritualism, and the creative powers of individual thought took up the majority of her time by the 1920s, to the point where Susan established the Lawrence Metaphysical Center in 1924, later reorganised as the Lawrence Center of Constructive Thinking.

Although she was exposed to successful business dealings through her father's pursuits, Susan was never able to apply them to her own affairs. Towards the end of her life she had considerable assets but was either unaware of them, or unable to deal with them, as they were never put to her advantage. As she had no family or close friends to take care of her, her affairs were neglected. She apparently felt that it was too costly to keep the house and hence, moved into the White Cottage, west of the railroad tracks, in 1928. Her quality of life suffered to the point where she was declared incompetent in the early 1940s and committed to an institution. Susan's possessions were catalogued and auctioned in 1943, three years before her death. She died on February 20, 1946, at the age of 83.

Susan Lawrence Dana (1862-1946), in front of her house, c1920. The dress was from an earlier era.

FRANK LLOYD WRIGHT'S BACKGROUND

Springfield is the well known home of the United States' sixteenth president, Abraham Lincoln. How appropriate it is that when Wright was born on June 8, 1867, he was given the middle name of Lincoln. For much of his early life he was known as Frank L Wright, but it was not until his architectural practice was established that he formalised the usage with the old family name of Lloyd, and became Frank Lloyd Wright.

Wright is internationally recognised as one of the most industrious architects. Success may seem to have come easily to him but he apparently spent many long nights working at home while employed at Adler & Sullivan's office, and kept regular office hours as well as hours in the evenings, and on Saturdays after his Oak Park practice opened in 1893. He built over four hundred buildings and designed nearly a thousand during his eighty-year career. When asked why he designed predominantly houses, rather than other types of buildings, he responded by saying that is what his clients asked him to do.

The Dana House is a residential interpretation of the design for the Hillside Home School (8703). The school is located in Spring Green and was designed just before the Dana House. The south facades of the buildings are nearly identical. They include an arched door to the right with tall windows above, and piers at the sides of the windows. A lower section connects a pavilion to the west end of the house.

Why Susan Lawrence Dana believed Wright could fulfil her requirements on the scale she anticipated is unknown. Perhaps it was Wright's ability as a salesman to talk her into such extensive remodelling and addition. He had undertaken several other remodellings before the approximate date of their first meeting somewhere in 1901 or 1902. These included his own house and studio, the H P Young House (9507), Charles E Roberts House (9603), H R Goodrich House (9601), and the Edward R Hill House (0102), all of Oak Park, as well as the Edward C Waller House (9902) of River Forest. It seemed that Wright would take on any design project of any size.

Concurrent with the Dana House, Wright was completing the design of the Francis W Little House (0009) in Peoria. There are so many similar features between the two houses that it would not be unreasonable to consider the Little House a scaled-down version of the Dana House (as with the Tomek [0711] and the Robie [0908] Houses). The living room, furniture, front door and art glass were nearly interchangeable. Two cabinets, one of all drawers and one of a secretary from the Little House were thought for some time to be from the Dana House.

Wright and others in his studio must have made many visits to the Dana House and the nearby Little House. It also provided a convenient excuse to travel on to St Louis and visit its influential 1904 World's Fair, but there are no records from

Frank Lloyd Wright
This is probably a self-portrait of 1902. Wright had a darkroom in his Oak Park studio above the vault on the south side of the drafting room.

Crane Library, Quincy, Massachusetts, 1880
Built by Henry Hobson Richardson, this photograph shows the interior of the library.

Bradley House, Kankakee
The porch extends directly into the grounds from the living room, unlike the one from the Gallery of the Dana House.

Oak Park Playroom and Dana Dining Room
In 1895, Wright built this addition to his Oak Park home. The barrel-vaulted room is much smaller than similar rooms in the Dana House and the skylight is missing in the Dana example.

Wright's office, Susan's papers, nor notations from the participants such as Griffin and Drummond, to certify this supposition.

Wright was well-versed in the use of many architectural elements and geometric shapes. The arch, which was used throughout the Dana House in plan and elevation, could have been the influence of the most prominent architect of Wright's youth, Henry Hobson Richardson, who used the arch extensively in doors, entrances and ceilings of major rooms. Richardson's buildings included classroom buildings at Harvard and small town libraries around Boston. Sullivan continued this tradition in his Transportation Building at the Chicago World's Fair of 1893, the Getty Tomb, the Auditorium Building in Chicago, and many other buildings. Wright's own playroom of 1895 is very similar to the dining room of the Dana House with brick walls and banded barrel vaults. The spatial extension by mural, window and borrowed space is found in both examples.

Wright's use of materials was well-established before he was commissioned to design the Dana House. Roman brick was used on an inside wall at the entrance of his first commission, the Winslow House (9305). Friezes on the Winslow, Heller (9606) and Husser (9901) Houses are more Sullivan in design than the 'art deco' abstraction of the Dana House. The Willits House (0208) of 1901 had a much freer pinwheel plan and was on a much larger site.

The Dana House was not the only case where Wright built a larger house around a smaller one. The Beachy House (0601) on Forest Avenue in Oak Park, Wright's own street, incorporates a house in a similar fashion to the Dana House. His attorney, Sherman Booth of Glencoe, asked Wright to do much the same with his house. Except for possibly the Hayashi House (1702), it was the last time Wright included another building on a design scheme.

It is somewhat surprising that the opulent Dana House has not received more attention over the years. This may be a result of the owners not allowing entry to the building or because there are so many more Wright buildings concentrated in a large metropolitan area nearby, Chicago, where a third of Wright's work is located. Now, since it is open for public tours, it may begin to receive the recognition and respect it deserves.

Wright's career continued for another fifty-five years after the Dana House. As mentioned earlier, it included many houses, but other works of major importance were also built, such as the Unity Temple (0611), Midway Gardens (1401), Imperial Hotel (1509), National Life Insurance Building, Johnson Wax (3601), and Guggenheim Museum. His own residences in Oak Park, Spring Green and Scottsdale rank as high as any he designed for his clients.

Wright was always exploring the capacity of a two by four, always experimenting with new geometries and artistic complexities. His capacity for inspiration was as large as his energy to make an idea into something tangible. His designs were often held inside his mind until every last detail was completed. It was then transferred to paper for others to see, understand and build. If he saw opportunities which could not be realised in his mind, he would alter the plan (even during construction) just to create the best building possible. The clients were not always in agreement with this procedure, but Wright pushed them as far as possible so that they would have as much of his genius as possible in their house. Often this would be the only house they would ever build, as with Susan Dana. Many, thankfully, gained so much from the experience, costly as it may have been, that they employed his services many times.

Wright's inspired constructions at the Dana House were never equalled. This house contains the best of many types of design, including the fountain art glass doors, entry fanlight, dining room butterfly lamps, table lamps, tall back dining chair, square-leg dining table, print table and music cabinet. Only the D D Martin House (0405) of Buffalo has come close to competing with the designs in the Dana House.

THE DANA HOUSE SITE

According to local lore, there were at least two provisions to Rheuna Lawrence's will that could not be broken by his daughter, Susan. The first was that the Italianate Lawrence House could not be torn down and the second was that Susan's main residence had to be on the site of the Lawrence House. This may explain why in the photographs showing the construction of the Dana House, the Lawrence House still stands within the new Wright-designed walls, and why the outline of the Lawrence House is delineated in all the plans, even in the Wasmuth drawings of 1910.

These two provisions, whether they were from the will or self-imposed by Susan Dana, confined Wright in many ways. He did not have the large open site of the Willits (0208) or Coonley (0803) Houses near Chicago, or the Martin House (0405) in Buffalo, New York. It obviously hampered his ability to devise an innovative sweeping interior that would surpass the one he created a year earlier for Mr Willits in Highland Park. His remedy for this may have been to date the Dana House before the Willits House and even before the Bradley House (0002) of Kankakee, Illinois. In the 1910 Wasmuth drawings, the Dana House was noted as having been built in 1899. One can only speculate on each of these points until the will, Susan's letters or copies of those from Wright are located.

The levels of the Dana House are dictated by those of the earlier Lawrence House. The floor of the main level aligns with that of the parlour of the Lawrence House, which remained intact in Wright's work. Wright's sensitivity to proportion resulted in the earth berm at the edge of the site, making the Dana House appear to be built on a slightly elevated table of land. The berm device would also make the Dana House appear to be more imposing than if it had been built at curb level.

The brick wall, while enclosing the backyard, extends the building in much the same way as the low walls of the D D Martin House (0405). It also gives much needed privacy to the west yard, the border of which is located within fifteen feet of both a busy street to the south and a mainline railroad track to the west. The wall obscures the former Lawrence barn located in the northwest corner of the lot and duplicates the curve of the breakfast bay in a small paddock on the barn's east side. The barn, now called the Carriage House, is used as a visitors' centre which includes offices and the Sumac Shop.

There never were great vistas of the prairie from the house because the sites across Lawrence Avenue are higher and were built-up before Wright began work on the house.

The main exit from the house to the backyard is through a set of doors behind the entry fountain. These wide stairs lead down

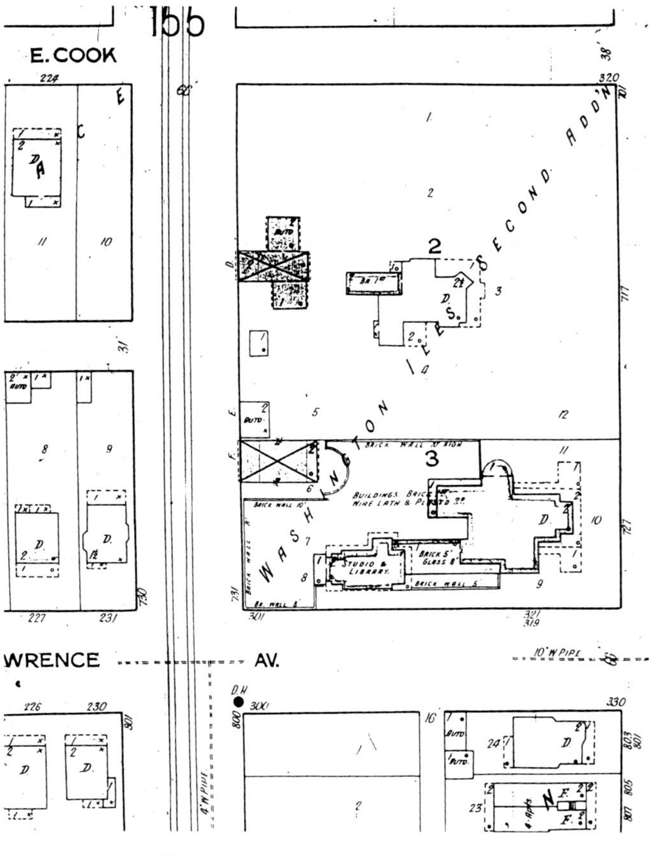

Sandborn map of Lawrence Site

This map clearly shows the original house and the two additions in the east centre of the lot. The numbers show the original subdivision of the land by Mr Washington Ile into twelve lots, four large and eight small. At the west end of Rheuna's lot is another. This lot includes the White Cottage and the stable, or barn, in the northwest corner.

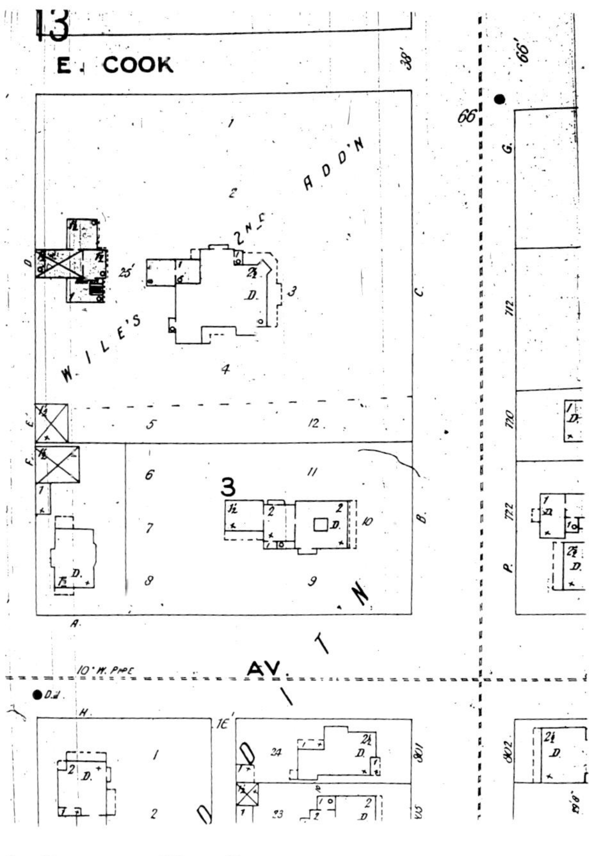

Sandborn map of Dana Site

The site is the same with the alterations by Wright noted in detail, as in room descriptions and heights of brick walls. This map shows the enlargement of the barn and the relocation of the White Cottage, west of the tracks. The west yard is nearly the same size as the site of the original White Cottage. *Both maps courtesy of Rich L Branom.*

White Cottage
The wall to the right is the rear wall of the Dana House. Looking across the railroad tracks toward the dome of the State Capitol is the White Cottage.

to the long fish pond, past flower beds and then to the north and west lawns. The Thomas' filled in the pond, creating another flower bed. The backyard is flat with no additional berms, steppes, cascades or vertical definition.

On an 1892 map of Springfield, the site of the Dana House is shown on the corner of 4th Street and Wright Street. Wright Street ran from Pasfield, east to 6th Street. An 1894 Plat Book of Sangamon County showed Douglas Street instead of Wright Street past 12th Street on the east. An 1898 *Illinois Capital Illustrated* indicates Wright Street west of Pasfield to West Grand and Douglas from Pasfield all the way east. *The Street Map of Springfield, Illinois*, dated July 1905 does not show Wright Street at all and the former Douglas Street is now shown as Lawrence Avenue from east to west. The street was renamed to commemorate Rheuna Lawrence and his contribution to Springfield.

Within the context of Springfield, the site has many advantages. Governor's Mansion and the State Capitol are one and three blocks north respectively. The house is also within walking distance of Lincoln's Home, three blocks to the northeast. Being so close to the centre of town it would have been easy to walk to and from gatherings.

Now the site is confined by smaller houses to the south and west, with an apartment building a few feet from its northern boundary. This was not the case in 1902. The Dana House sits on a site 125 feet by 240 feet (about a half acre) and occupies six lots, from numbers 6 to 11, which had been subdivided earlier. The lot was subdivided itself with a 60 foot by 125 foot parcel at the west end. The White Cottage occupies this lot. The barn was located in the extreme northwest corner. This lot is designated as plot A, with the remainder, Rhuena's House, being plot B. The site to the north (about an acre) had a very large house set in the centre.

The Lawrence barn was shown to be square in the 1896 map, and nearly twice as large in a 1906 edition, after the Wright remodelling. There was a six foot wide shed about twelve feet to the south, nearly touching the back porch of the cottage. This shed is not shown in the 1906 plan.

After the White Cottage was moved west across the tracks, it was set about ten feet further back from the street than on its original site behind Rheuna's house.

There were predominantly large, well-landscaped houses along 4th Street, most of which were built before the turn of the century. By comparison, the Rhuena Lawrence house was quite modest. The Matteson House was considered by many to rival the largest and most elaborate of the territory, which included Chicago. It was located on 4th Street opposite the Governor's Residence and unfortunately burned down on an extremely cold night in 1873. At the northeast corner of 4th and Cook stood the Italianate villa of C M Smith, which included a four-

Dana House Backyard Fence

This photo was taken from the west side of the railroad tracks, in front of the White Cottage. The yard enclosed by the brick wall is the original site of the White Cottage. The building with the black metal fire stairs is the Coachouse to the Dana property.

storey tower. Immediately to the north of the Lawrence House was the Hay House, originally built in the early 1860s. It was remodelled in the 1880s for the daughter and her husband Mr Brown and was subsequently called the Hay-Brown House. It was demolished in 1934. The YMCA is now on the corner of 4th and Cook.

The proximity to the main railroad line to the west of the Dana House had a very detrimental effect on the building as well as its occupants. The 1896 plan shows a single set of tracks which had been extended to a double set by 1906. The trains were likely to come through at any time of the day or night, disturbing sleep, music or just concentration. The disturbance came in the form of noise as well as vibrations, as long lines of heavy train cars would shake the ground, the structure, and its contents. The sulphur from the smokestacks employed on the coal burning trains, still operating into the 1950s, caused deterioration to the mortar as well as the copper trim work. When the Thomas' took the house in the 1940s, a knife could easily pierce the mortar joints. The mortar had deteriorated to such a point that it was said to be 'standing on sand' and the Thomas' fortunately undertook the formidable task of repointing the entire building.

Little is known about the landscaping of the site. It is likely that Walter Burley Griffin may have helped in selecting and locating the plants, but no documents have been located. It is not known if there was any live sumac on the site as none of the renderings or photographs show any evidence of this. Since the major motif of the house is an abstracted sumac, which is expressed in many of the art glass windows, the frieze and the dining room murals, it might be expected that a specimen may be highlighted somewhere. Sumac is not usually considered a garden species but more of a wild weed and it may have been decided that it would be better to leave it in the wild.

A small frame house was built on the southwest corner of the Lawrence site just east of the railroad tracks. It is believed that it was built for Susan and Edwin Dana around 1893 when they moved back to Springfield after living in Minneapolis, Chicago and possibly elsewhere. At the time of the Wright construction, it was moved west across the Illinois Central tracks and Susan lived in the house from 1928 until the 1940s. No records show the name of the designer of the cottage nor the actual date of its construction. There is some evidence, in the form of a basement buff-coloured fireplace, that Wright carried out some design work. The house is now known as 'The White Cottage' and is used for support services by the State in servicing the Dana House.

Over the years the Dana House site has been home to many trees, including the magnificent American Elm. These have been cut down due to age and disease, but will hopefully be replaced in the new plan.

THE DANA HOUSE BACKGROUND

The Rheuna Lawrence House was a fine example of a typical four square Italianate house, complete with a large windowed cupola, or lantern, at the peak of the hipped roof. It had two additions at the back, one of which included a two-storey bay on the south side and a pantry. While not in the least ostentatious, the house had a conservative number of roof brackets at the modest overhang of the roof, which was composed of sawn cedar shingles. It has been described as a sixteen-room house. It was constructed of red brick though the two photographs reveal a painted finish. The first floor window on the south elevation is shown with the shutters closed. This is a blind window because the stairs to the second floor ran behind it and hence, the window could not be opened. The bathrooms were located in the northwest corner of the second floor in a similar location as the current plumbing.

The original house was nearly square, with approximate measurements of 32 feet by 34 feet, and about the size of the 1906 Wright design for the 'Fireproof House for $5,000'. A remodelling of a similar sized Victorian house is the Copeland House of Oak Park. This house, which is just south of Wright's own home on Forest Avenue, was remodelled in 1909.

Before Mr Lawrence purchased the property in 1868, a house existed on the site that appears to have been built c1854 by D E Rucket. It is unknown what the Rucket House looked like. The land was owned prior to that by forty-two year old Abraham Lincoln in 1851, a Springfield attorney, land speculator and later the sixteenth US President.

Most of the Lawrence house, including the two additions, was incorporated into the Dana House. Wright's familiar freeflow planning and spatial layout is hence absent. This does not mean that the result is not as spectacular as other houses of the era, but only that it is unusual in the development of his work.

The first scheme Wright proposed to Susan Lawrence Dana was similar to what was built, but with two dramatic exceptions: the entrance hall and the dining room were initially designed differently. In the first plan, the latter was a single storey room with a bedroom above, ending where the current north bay begins. A large fireplace was located at the south end of the room with a cloakroom and powder room south and adjacent to it. The entrance hall did rise two storeys but a blank wall stood opposite the front door. A fireplace was located at the northwest corner of the reception hall. In the basement, one area where the bowling alley and the vault are located was not even excavated. The library was a waiting room with a large darkroom at the west end. There is no mention of Susan's interest in photography but it must have been significant as such a large space was devoted to it.

The second, altered plan, shows the building in much the same design as it now exists. Interestingly, the fountain in the reception area is only pencilled-in, as an obvious afterthought. The fireplace, which is now opposite the front door, was relocated about a foot to the north, allowing for more room in the reception area. The bedroom that formerly occupied the space on the second storey over the dining room was relocated to the bathroom area, which was duly reconfigured.

It is worth noting that in both plans a tree is shown in the middle of the south porch. This is a feature that Wright used in two other buildings, his own studio in Oak Park which Susan may have seen, and later in the porch of his secretary's house, Isabel Roberts, in nearby River Forest. From the photographs of the early construction, it appears that the idea was disregarded and the tree removed.

While Susan owned the house there were few changes. The house was essentially abandoned during the fifteen or so years before the Thomas' bought it. Mr Thomas found pigeons living in the house and after the clean-up, Wright suggested using a nearly black stain on the damaged wood to obscure the damage. As mentioned previously, the sulphur from the coal-burning trains that ran next to the building had turned the brick's mortar to sand. A careful job of matching the original raked horizontal joints was carried out during the tuckpointing. Very little was done other than maintenance work while the Thomas' owned the house from 1942 to 1981. They introduced air-conditioning and additional lighting, mostly fluorescent, in order to make the building more functional as a publishing office, but all additions were very carefully planned and executed so not to alter the building. The original red tile roof had been previously coated with aluminium paint and was hence replaced with identical red tiles at tremendous expense.

After the State of Illinois purchased the property, a complete remodelling was undertaken, which took three years and over $5,000,000. All the furniture, windows and wall surfaces were renovated and the exterior plaster frieze was painted and reinstalled; storm windows with bronze glass were installed over the art glass; a new fire and security system was installed in a non-intrusive manner; and the entire coachouse was redesigned to accommodate new HVAC, offices, bookshop and a visitors' centre.

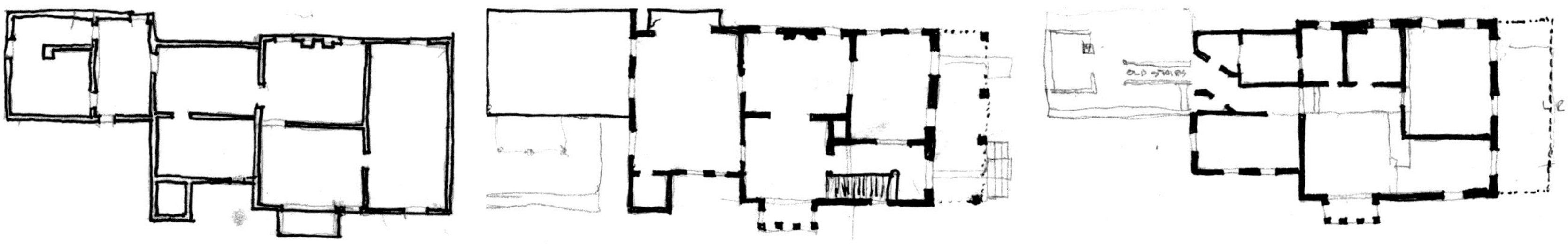

Lawrence House, First and Second Floor Plans
These plans were developed from the original Dana House drawings and show the approximate disposition of the rooms.

Rheuna Lawrence House
It is believed that Rheuna Lawrence built this house in the late 1860s. The architectural style reflects this theory. Photographs show that the house was not opulent and was of average size. Despite adequate space for a carriage drive in front or to the side of the house, Mr Lawrence apparently chose not to build one. The White Cottage is to the far left and a frame gazebo is nearby. *Photo c1880 from the Archives of the Dana-Thomas House, State Historic Site.*

Dana House, Construction A
This construction photograph and the one below, Construction B, were taken within a few days of each other – this is evident by the progress of the brickwork. Photograph A shows an edge of the Lawrence House to the right. It even reveals some of the wallpaper used inside. The projecting boards are the former floorboards of the south bay of the house. The White Cottage and construction tent are beyond. The gazebo was moved from the yard to the Lawrence Avenue parkway at the left. The stairs to the right of the gazebo lead from the front door to the porch between Mother Lawrence's bedroom and the Gallery. Once the house was completed the same view would have been seen from the living room doors across the reception to the fountain. *DH 89.F.2.6 from the Archives of the Dana-Thomas House, State Historic Site.*

Dana House, Construction B
The area on the immediate right is the end of the bowling alley, from where the stairs lead up to the Gallery. The Library floor was built on the two rows of bricks left of centre. The original Lawrence barn is in the background to the right. The White Cottage had not been moved across the tracks at this point and was probably the home of Susan and her mother during construction. Unfortunately, there are no photographs of the work with the barrel vaults of the dining room and the Gallery. *DH 89.F.2.5 from the Archives of the Dana-Thomas House, State Historic Site. Winter 1902-03.*

Dana House, Construction C
Taken from the north-east corner of the lot, the photograph shows more additions to the original Lawrence House. *DH 89 F.2.4 from the Archives of the Dana-Thomas House, State Historic Site. Winter 1902-03.*

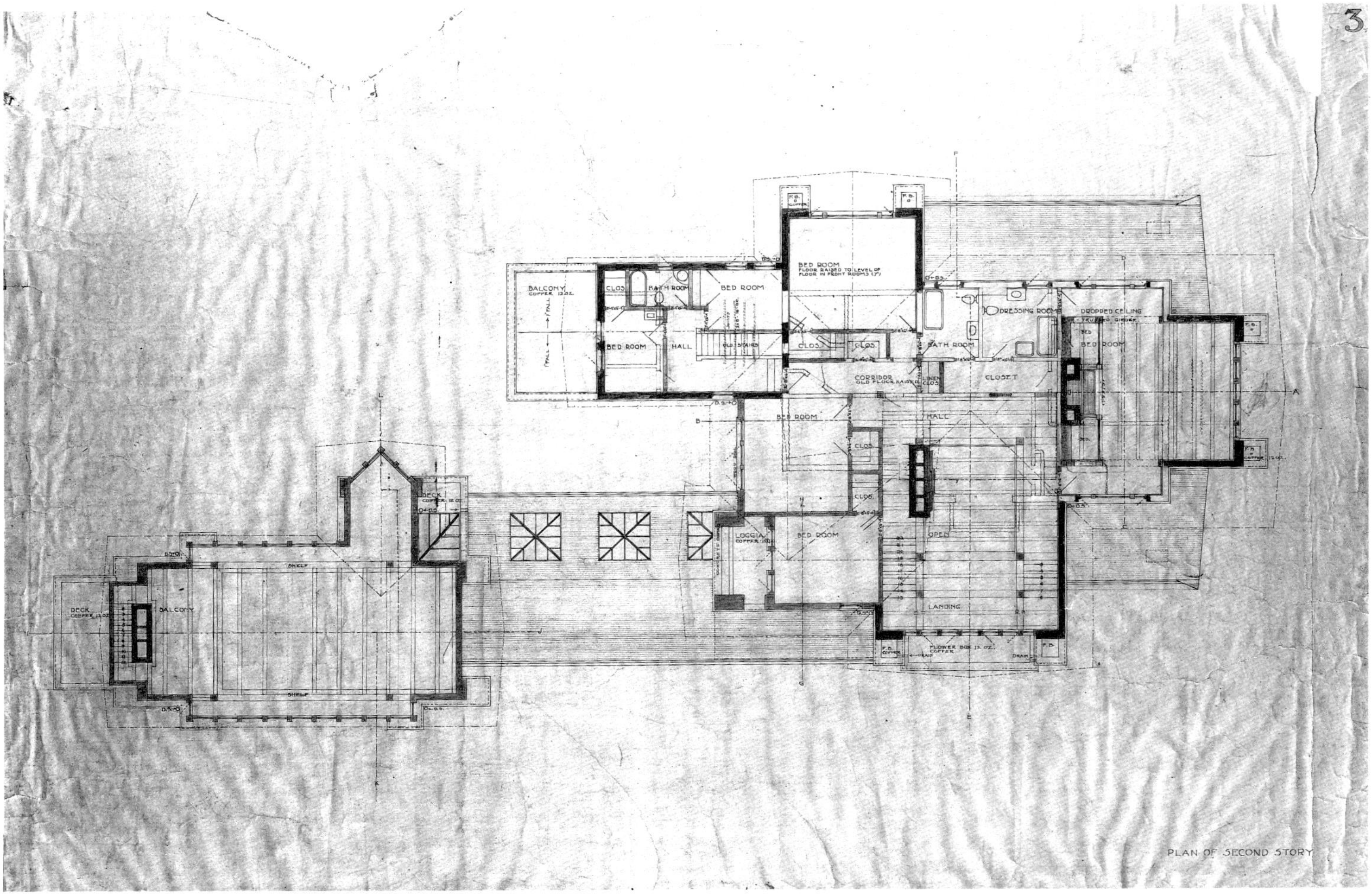

Second Floor Plan, design 1 above, design 2 below

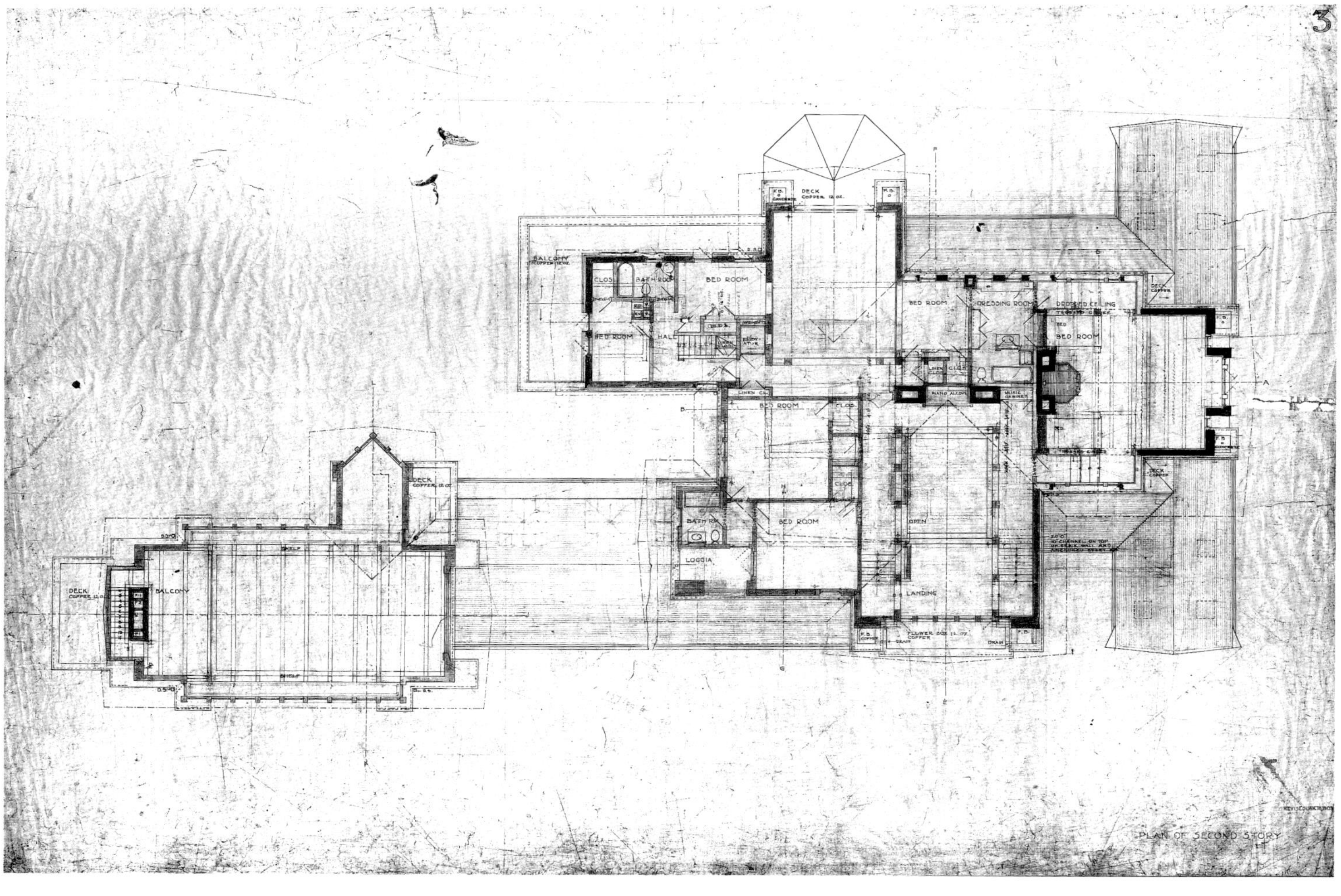

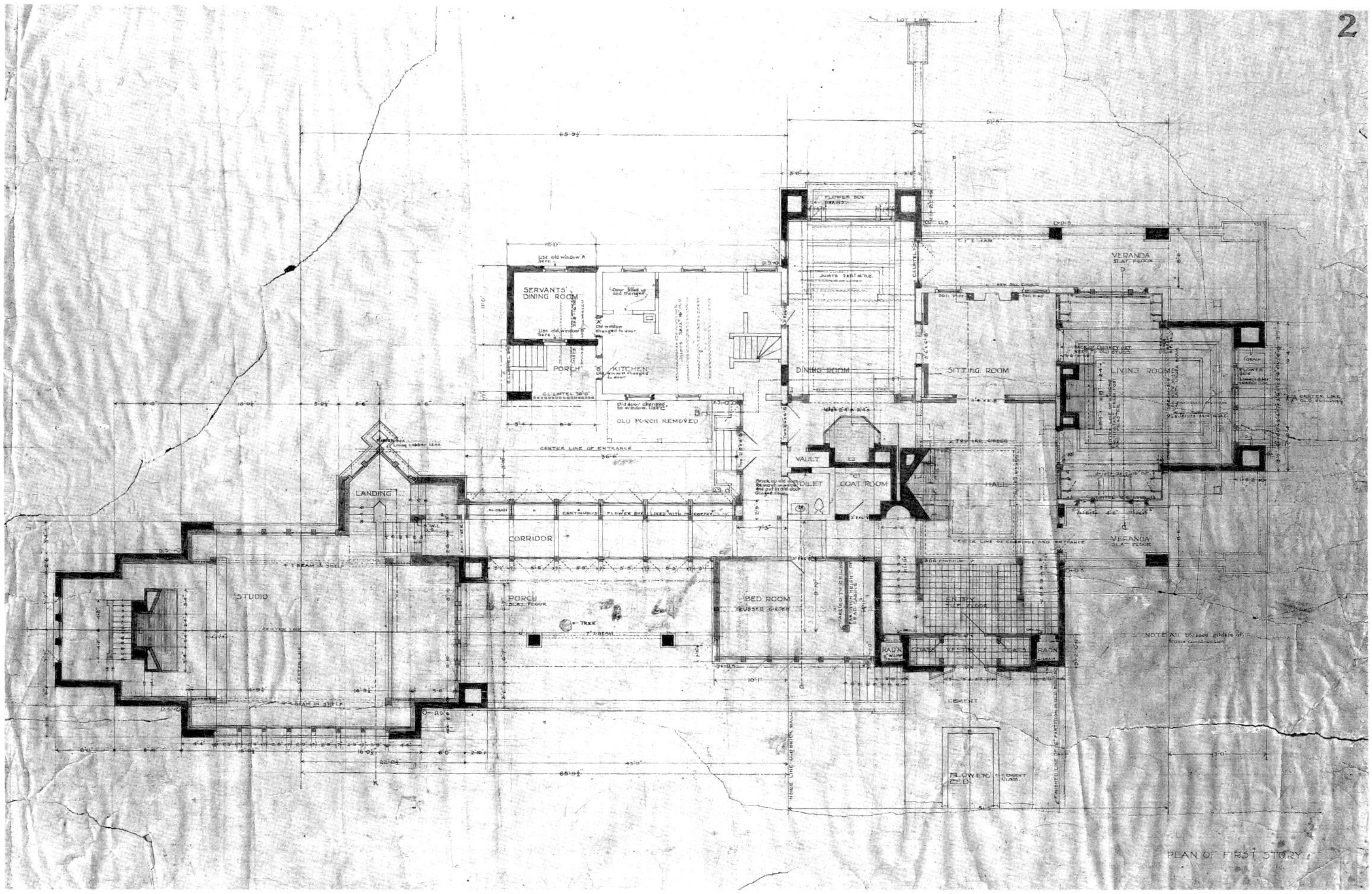

First Floor Plan, design 1 above, design 2 below

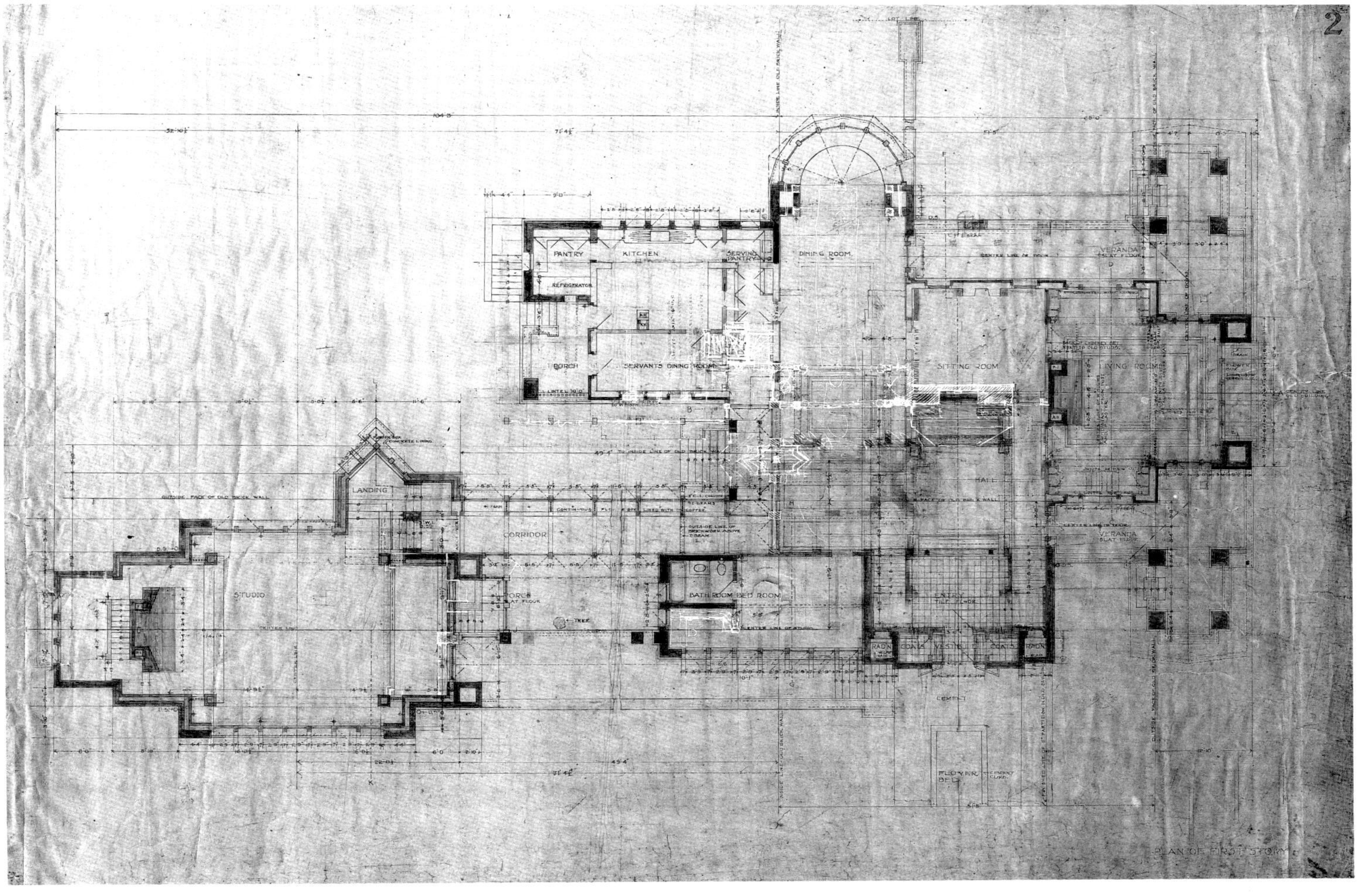

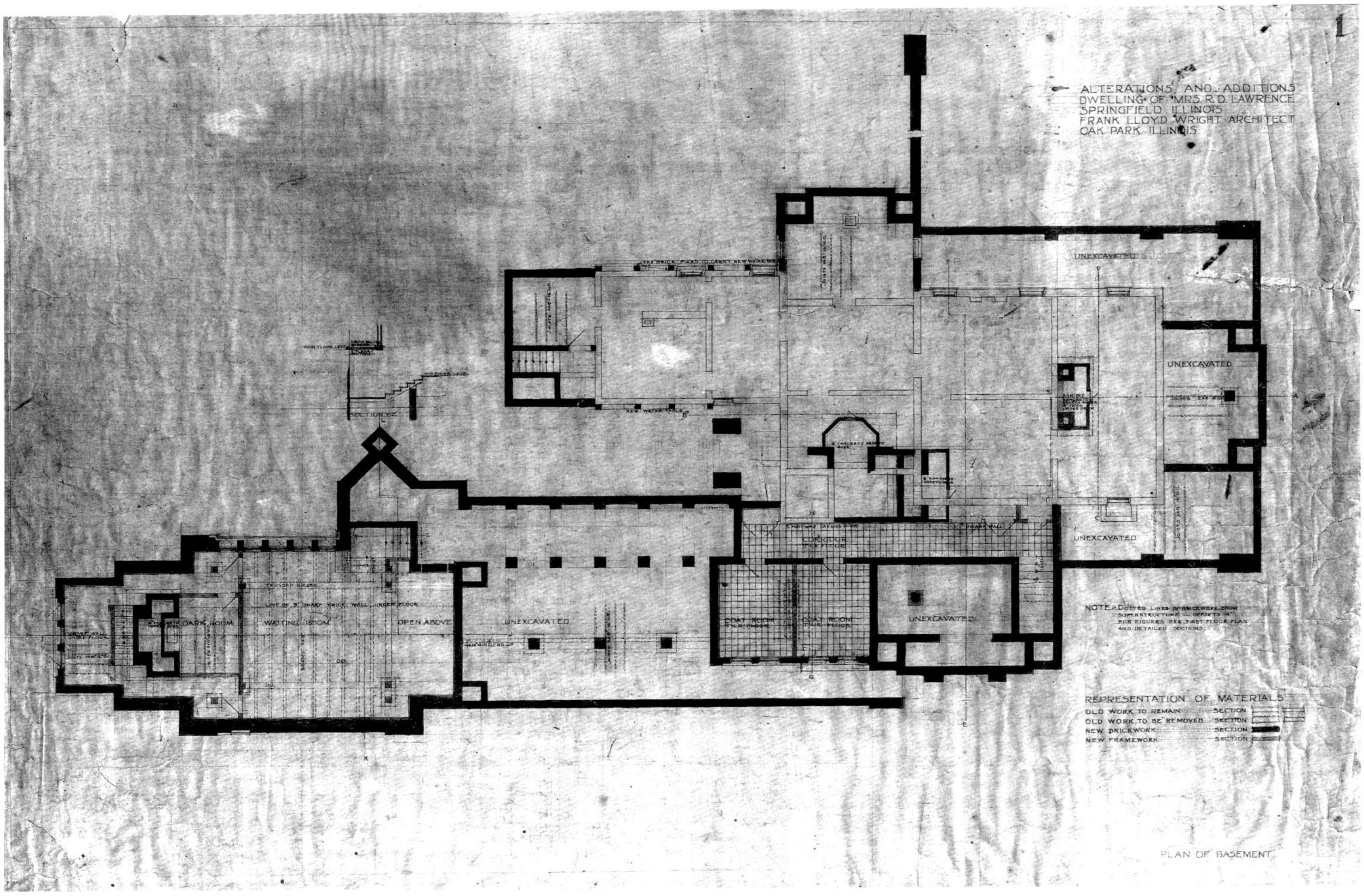

Basement Floor Plan, design 1 above, design 2 below

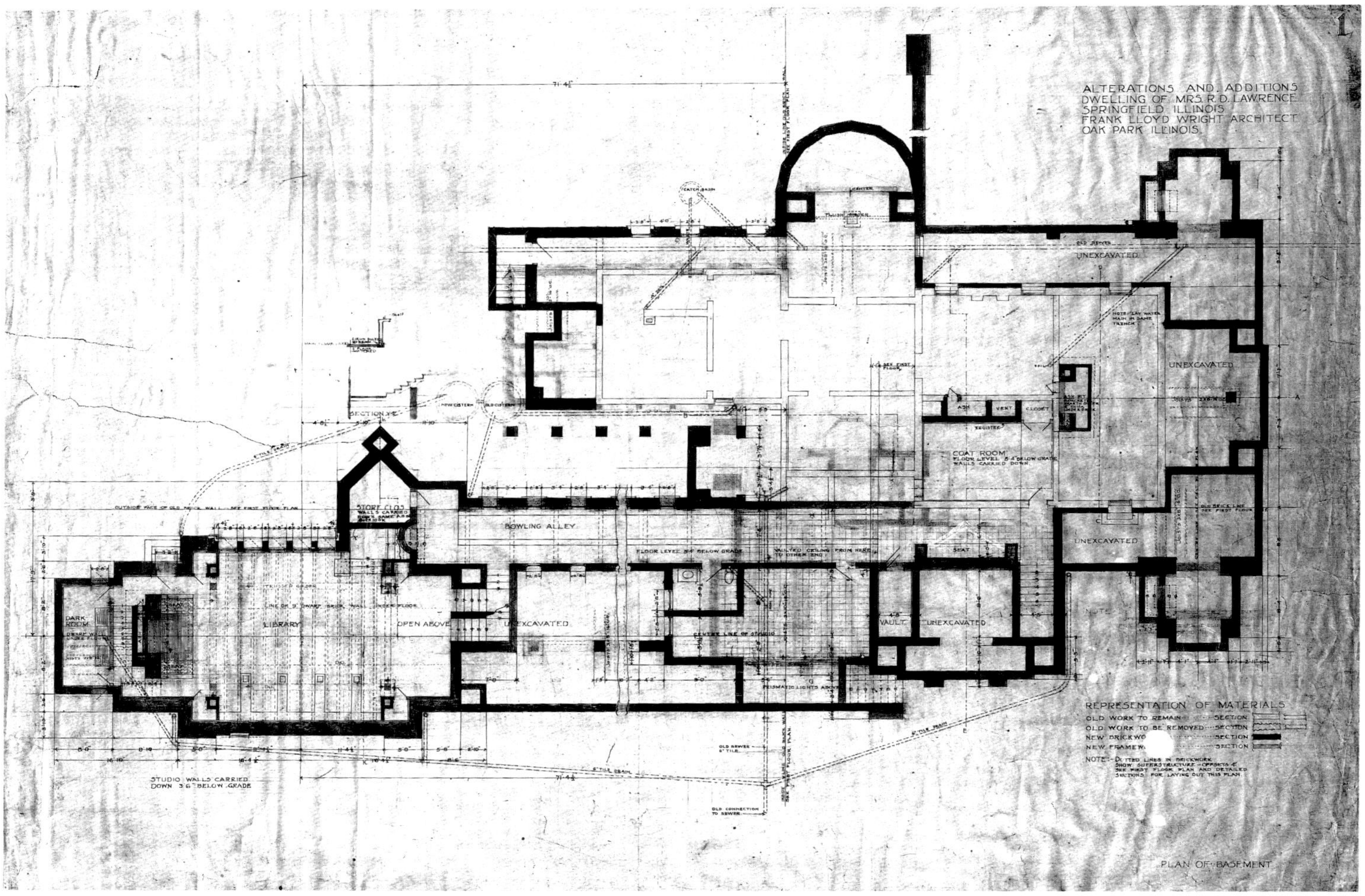

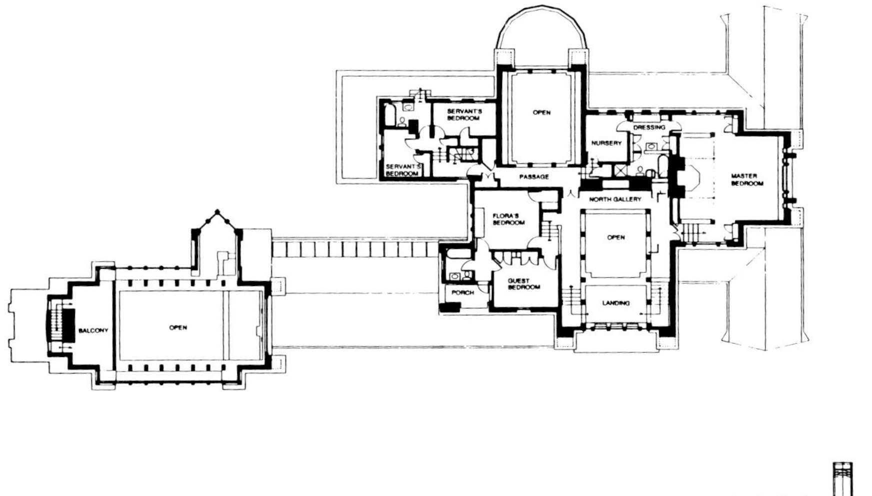

SECOND FLOOR PLAN

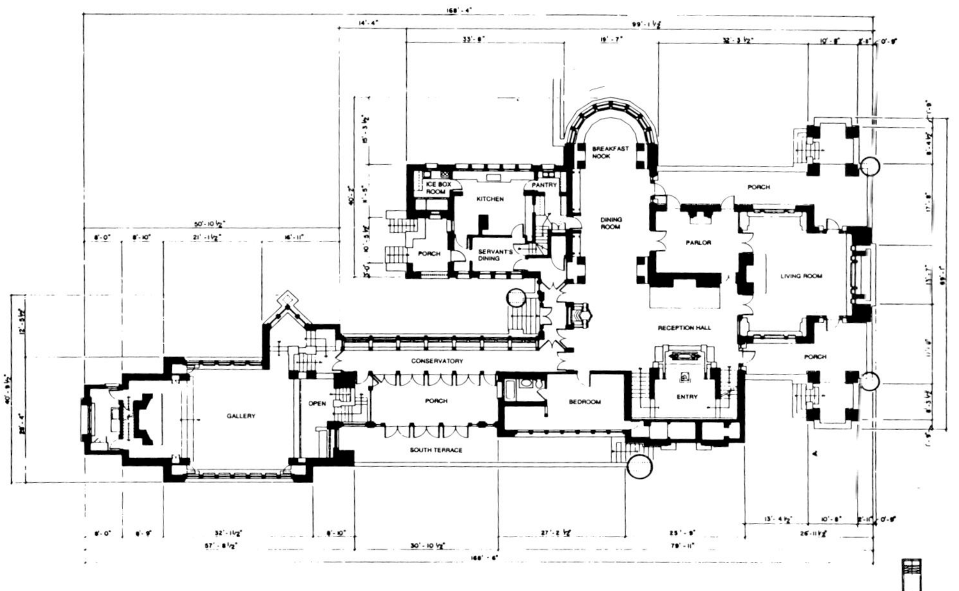

FIRST FLOOR PLAN

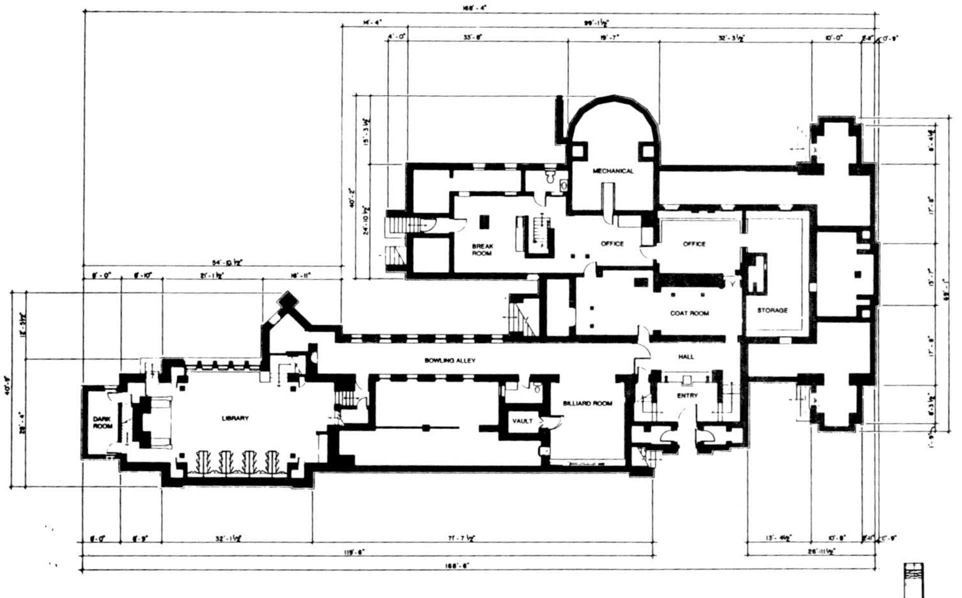

BASEMENT FLOOR PLAN

Existing floor plans, HABS drawn by James G Hollis, 1984.

BUILDING EXTERIOR

The Dana House, like all of Wright's buildings, was developed so that form followed function. This does not literally imply that one can determine the function of the interior space by examining the exterior form, but that the function is provided for by the form. As a result, most of Wright's buildings are not symmetrical.

Few of Wright's Prairie era buildings had gables. Most of the designs were intended to downplay their height to the street. The Dana House gables make the entrance appear to be taller than the space inside, which is only two storeys high, while the facade is three storeys. Small additions at the ends of the eaves imply an oriental influence. By comparing this to the gable of the Bradley House (0002) which does not have the small additions, it shows that architectural features of this size have a great impact on the overall impression.

The Dana House is one of only four Wright Houses with a plaster frieze. The others include the 1893 Winslow House (9305) in a Sullivanesque style; the Heller House (9606) with a design that includes human figures; and the Husser House (9901). The Robert Irving House (1003) of Decatur and the Coonley House (0803) of Riverside both have partial ceramic tile friezes. The Dana House frieze is a development of the Sullivanesque designs, like others of this pattern, but looks forward to Art Deco. The broken lines become a lightning bolt that was popularised in the Art Deco period. The original colour was never described but we can assume that it was similar to other Wright friezes, which were approximately the same colour as the brick used on the walls of the houses.

Unlike the vast majority of Wright's houses, the entrance to the Dana House is prominent and is approached directly from the street. While most of Wright's clients were seeking privacy, Susan Lawrence Dana enjoyed entertaining and often invited a great number of people into her home. The arched doorway was set at street level as was Oak Park's Thomas House (0106) which had been built a year previously, and the Heurtley House (0204), a year later. Both have powerful arched entrances. The Little House (0009) of Peoria, of the same date as the Dana House, has a simplified arched fanlight at its front door on a slightly smaller scale than the Dana House. The tall windows above the door in the latter indicate a significant space within.

The porches on the east side of the building were enlarged and reoriented from the first design. This may have been in order to catch the occasional breeze, but they also make the building appear much larger.

It is not known why the Gallery is a separate pavilion. This set-off section of the building is part of a string of designs starting with the 1894 Bagley House library (9401). The Bagley library is identical to the library of his own 1897 Oak Park Studio. The separate pavilion idea may be more closely related to the development of Hillside Home School, designed just prior to the Dana House.

The brick used to build the Dana House is a creamy grey Roman brick. In the changing light of Springfield it can appear cold grey or quite yellow. The concrete base and cap with the frieze incorporates the same motif as the one used on the Winslow House, Wright's first independent commission ten years earlier. The red of the tiled roof is the strongest exterior colour, making all the other colours appear softer.

East Facade

The east facade is symmetrical, an unusual feature in a Wright building. The north and south porches may have been added in the second design in order to create the impression of horizontality. One of the most interesting features of the east facade is the art glass pattern, with all the window openings comprising a single design.

In contrast to the street facade, the yard elevations are less studied. They do not make as harmonious a composition, as windows seem to poke out in unrefined locations, leaving an impression of being left-over parts from the rest of the exterior.

Detail of East Facade

View of Backyard

Old South Facade

Hillside Home Schoo

Old Entrance

East Facade

View to the East

View to the West

Frieze and Eave detail

View to the West

Front Door Detail

Detail of Flower Urn

Base and Wall Detail

Gallery

BUILDING INTERIOR

BASEMENT

The Dana House is one of two Wright-designed residences with any finished basement rooms which were intended for use as more than storage space. The Darwin D Martin House (0405) is the second example. The library, bowling alley and coat storage in the Dana House were fully finished for daily use. A bowling alley is rare in any residence, but it is the only recorded interior sports or athletic facility in a Wright building. It is often pointed out on public tours that lore has it that duck pins, smaller than standard bowling pins, were used. Near the bowling alley there is a small closet that still contains wine racks for wine storage. It is not very large and seems to have been for the use of the occupants rather than storage for the large receptions and dinners. The location of this space is unusual since it is not at the dining room end of the house, and because the storage area is small, it is obviously not for the storage of wine for receptions in the Gallery above.

Many rooms in Wright-designed buildings have been noted as libraries. Wingspread, the Johnson House (3703) in Racine, Wisconsin, is the only other house to have planned double-sided bookshelves for the storage of books in the same manner as libraries, but the Johnson House bookracks were eliminated in a later scheme. A stairway offered direct entry from the outside porch to the library, so that children or other visitors did not have to walk through the house in order to reach the library. The space created at the entrance and stairway is a three-storey space rising to the arched ceiling of the gallery above. Behind the fireplace, at the west end, was the darkroom complete with a sink. At the east end of the bench seat along the north wall of the library, is a brick base that contains a secret compartment, thought by some to have been used for cooling wine. It is assumed that this would have contained something more valuable than what was in the vault at the other end of the basement, but what that was, no one knows.

Under the entrance to the front porch and to the left of the front door is a space with sidewalk prisms and an arched ceiling. These prisms are the same as those developed by the Luxfer Prism Company where Wright was employed as the architectural consultant in the late 1890s. Adjacent to this is a large bank-like vault with its original steel door. The door is painted with information regarding the manufacturer of the vault and names of the family. There are old batteries inside which may have been used for the security system and/or the bell-and-call system installed in the house. The remainder of the space below the original Lawrence House was for storage and was left mostly unfinished. Now it is used for offices and document vaults.

The far east end of the corridor that contains the bowling alley is the lowest part of the entrance and reception area. It has a partially open ceiling with a frame containing art glass covered lights on the top as well as the bottom. Stairs lead up to the front door and the Flower in the Crannied Wall sculpture.

Bowling Alley

FIRST FLOOR

Entry

The entrance and reception area is the most complex and the most difficult to define. It extends vertically through three stories, and horizontally north from the entry door to the Lawrence Parlour (the Victorian Room), and west from the living room to the fernery. It contains a set of stairs from the front door to the reception and parlour level, a fireplace with tapered brick voussoirs, and two terracotta sculptures by Richard W Bock: the Flower in the Crannied Wall at the front door and the Moon Children fountain. The stairs continue up to the second floor, pausing at a landing above the front door. Balconies frame three sides of the third level and provide access to the bedrooms and an electric pump organ above the first floor fireplace. As there are no columns supporting the balcony, it appears to be suspended from the roof. The most spectacular art glass ever designed by Wright is installed in the doors to the Moon Children fountain. Added to the decoration and spatial complexity of the room, a single pedestal art glass lamp and a hammered copper urn created an overwhelmingly beautiful effect which cannot be comprehended in a single visit. All of this together produces a complex series of spaces within a single room.

Living Room

The living room is the least spectacular major public room of the entire ensemble. It is reminiscent of a fish bowl, having at least one door or window in each wall. The walls of the niches north and south of the fireplace contain the original front and side walls of the Lawrence House. The wood banding of the ceiling is typical of the period and similar to that of the Fricke House (0201) living room in Oak Park, completed the year before the Dana House. There are no early photographs of what this room looked like during Susan's lifetime. It seems to have been used by the family rather than for social functions.

Dining Room

The dining room is the most spectacular room of the house. While it is horizontally axial and linear, the vertical thrust of the vaulted ceiling is powerful. The metal ropes of the hanging butterfly lights on the four corners of the room draw the high arched ceiling and the seating level together. The seating level occurs below the sumac frieze. The lights could have been hung from brackets on the wall but that would have produced a different effect altogether. The thrust of the tall back dining chairs is offset by the dropping lights at the corners. The two are not opposed because the chairs thrust upwards in the centre of the room and the lights drop at the corners, thus establishing a harmony, rather than creating tension.

The dining room is not confined in the traditional sense by four walls. The two side walls are defined by the original Lawrence House. The extension of the dining room space occurs in four directions. First the north breakfast bay pushes under the sumac frieze where the ceiling is much lower and opens into a bright, fan-like space. Secondly, the room opens to the south, towards the fountain. This extension could be confined, if desired, by the drawing of the portiers, or drapes, at two separate locations between the brick columns. Thirdly, in the upper level, the space is not blunted by a plaster wall but is visually extended through the sumac lunette window. And fourthly, a south-facing balcony echoes the north lunette window. The substantial wood columns that support the frame and curtain rods within the opening to the balcony are very similar to a Japanese Tori gateway. The Niedecken murals add a quiet touch at the centre of all this action. The colours of the murals change with the lighting of the seasons, alternating between warm and golden, and cold and blue.

The location and arrangement of the furniture varied depending on the use. The smaller square tables could be set against the larger one and seat forty, or the small square table could seat four. There are three variations of dining chairs. The familiar tall back chair is the most common. The medium back chair may have been used at the smaller tables when separated from the larger table and in the breakfast bay to be less overwhelming. An armed tall back chair was situated at the end on occasions which required greater formality.

Victorian Room

This room is the parlour from Rheuna Lawrence's original Italianate house. It is in the same location within the original walls. There is speculation as to why this room was not remodelled as all the others were. It is likely that Susan Dana requested that it was to remain as a memorial to Mr Lawrence. It occupied about one fourth of the floor space of the original Lawrence House, but in comparison to the new rooms, it appears quite small. The colours seem appropriate to the origins of the room.

SECOND FLOOR

Mother's Bedroom

Mrs Lawrence died a few months after the completion of the house and it appears that this room was used mostly for storage or perhaps for Susan's clothing.

Guest Room and Cousin Flora's Bedroom

The rooms are airy and are fitted with their own bathroom and balcony.

Master Bedroom

This room is directly above the living room and is consequently the same size. Susan may have taken some comfort in the fact that the bed locations were within the original walls of the Lawrence House. While there is ample accommodation for books and smaller items, there is no storage room for her clothing. This may have been stored in the bedroom west and behind the master bathroom, but it has been suggested that clothes were, in fact, stored in the first floor bedroom, or even the coach house and brought over each day by the servants. The most puzzling aspect of the room is the original location of the free-standing dressers. With no early photos of the room and no notations on the drawings there is only speculation.

Master Bathroom

One cannot imagine more types of bathroom fixtures being available at the time. This room was one of two locations of bathrooms in the original Lawrence House. The second Lawrence bathroom was what is now the bedroom to the west of this bathroom.

Servants' Rooms

These were within the original Lawrence House. Traditionally, servants were usually housed in the basement or in the attic and rarely had the privilege of having a room with a balcony.

Living Room

Dining Room Breakfast Bay

Fricke House Interior

Victorian Room

Reception and Entrance

Reception and Entrance from the Dining Room

Conservatory-Fernery

Early photographs show Boston ferns thriving in this corridor that connects the reception with the Gallery. The skylights and the heated flower boxes are well suited to growing such ferns. A long trough along the windows was said to hold goldfish. The porch to the south would have been a very good suntrap where one could sit on the coldest winter day and enjoy the sun without worrying about the wind.

Gallery

Originally called the Studio on the drawings, it is now referred to as the Gallery. The Gallery is very similar in nature and in its structural formation to the living room of the second Francis Little House of 1913, formerly of Wayzata Minnesota and now a permanent exhibit at the Metropolitan Museum of Art in New York City. (Interestingly, the first Little House in Peoria was being designed and built concurrent with the Dana House.) Even the east-west orientation is the same. The north and south window walls are self-supporting. The weight of the roof and ceiling is carried by the arched truss that runs just inside the windows, allowing for larger windows.

The Gallery is the brightest room in the entire building, in sharp contrast to the otherwise Victorian light levels throughout the rest of the house. In reference to it being a studio, there is no evidence of it being a music, painting or photographic studio for Susan. It is believed to have been used for grand balls with dancing and music recitals, and later for her spiritual gatherings. The balcony above the west fireplace was for musicians. The elevated floor at the fireplace and under the balcony would have given a more enclosed feeling to the space as well as serving as a small stage for presentations. In the early photographs, the room was furnished sparsely.

Despite the spectacular architecture, the unique feature of this room is not the architecture but the art glass screen hanging in front of the semi-circular window in the east end of the vault. This is the only recorded use of art glass being hung inside a plate glass window. The art glass is in seven sections, hung from a wooden frame similar to the Tori-style frame in the dining room. It can be reached only with great difficulty because of the chasm caused by the exterior staircase to the porch at the east end that leads down to the basement library. Curiously, there is no direct access from this room to the grounds outside. The Bradley and Willits Houses both had porches accessed through doors from the main living rooms. It does seem unusual that there was no where to 'go out for a breath of fresh air' during these social events.

While not the largest house designed by Wright, it is the most complex and most skilfully decorated. The finest of Wright's decorative designs were executed for the Dana House in many areas including art glass, furniture, murals, sculpture, pottery and metalwork. The quality of design is not a factor of cost but perhaps more to do with inspiration and inclination. Wright was in a unique position with his client, Susan Lawrence Dana, and his artisans/craftsmen: John Ayers in connection with furniture, Linden Art Glass with the lamps and windows, George Niedecken with the mural, Richard W Bock with the sculpture and Miller with the metalwork. These designs were new at this date. Directed by Wright, this combined talent worked harmoniously. Together they were able to accomplish more than at any other time in their careers. Of Wright's favourite artists only Orlando Giannini appears not to have been involved.

Reception/Entry Balcony

Dining Room

Conservatory-fernery

Master Bathroom

Master Bedroom looking East

Master Bedroom looking West

Gallery

Gallery

FURNITURE

Entrance Hall

A rare photograph of the entry hall shows a spindle-sided chair on the lower right. This chair is missing, as are a few other examples from the Dana House. All other styles of furniture are represented in the house but this is the only one with no record of its whereabouts. The sculpture on the far left is also of unknown authorship. The curtains (known as portières) are believed to be of a yellow-green colour, similar to those of the D D Martin House (0405). The rugs on the floor are known to be brown. The tall copper weedholder to the right of centre and another from the house have never been located. The living room and bedrooms appear to have never been photographed. It would be most helpful if photographs like these could be located.

Photo courtesy of The Dana-Thomas House, The Illinois Historic Preservation Agency.

Entrance through the Front Door
OPPOSITE, ABOVE: The view through the front door sets up the scheme for the entire building. The built-in shelves on the left must originally have contained hats, gloves, scarves, umbrellas and other items. The thick cap trim and the running borders guide the eye and define the planes and spaces. Wood posts which hold up the sconces and act to frame the view without confining it, occur frequently in the Dana House, in the master bedroom, living room and gallery.

Entry Fireplace
OPPOSITE, BELOW AND ABOVE: The next level above the entrance contains the reception hall, living room and dining room. This fireplace is on the same centreline as the entrance door and is flanked by two large settles. On entering, the visitor is greetec by the sculpture.

Entry Fountain/Reception
BELOW: It is romantic to think that Mrs Dana would have spent her time reading or reflecting in a comfortable chair by the fountain, but it is more likely that this was simply an area which linked the entrance to the living and dining rooms. Furniture scattered about the area was a carry-over from Victorian times.

Dining Room

With the many alternatives in lighting, this room is capable of projecting several moods. When the lights are turned off, the room feels cool and cave-like. With the lights on, it changes to a bright sunny summer day that would be quite welcoming in the cold windy Springfield winters. Utilising the potential combinations of furniture arrangements, the dining room can feel as open as the prairies that surrounded the city or as crowded as the city itself. The arrangement shown is a more conventional one between the two extremes. The north end, with its low ceiling, is thought to be the breakfast area as this would be lit with more natural light than the rest of the dining room.

Gallery

Settles at Fireplace

OPPOSITE, ABOVE: These two settles are freestanding in a location that would normally have accommodated built-in furniture. The angle of the fireplace is paralleled by the angle of the ends of the settles and in some of the angles of the art glass ceiling light. These continue the freestanding versus built-in scheme which was seen at the entry fireplace. The fabrics are not the original ones.

Gallery

OPPOSITE, BELOW: As with all of Wright's barrel-vaulted rooms, one end has a balcony to physically extend the space outside the limits of the room. At the other end is either a mural (as in Wright's playroom, 9307) or an arched window opposite the balcony. In the same style as the playroom, there are bays on the longitudinal sides of the room, with large windows which extend past the spring line, piercing the vault itself. The floor does not extend to the far wall, stopping short to accommodate a stairway to the library below. The large settle has a bookcase on the back. The low back chairs along each bay were originally from the Dana Memorial Library in the nearby Lawrence School.

Master Bedroom

ABOVE: Why these massive, heavy pieces were not built-in remains as much a mystery as their original location in the room. They are a larger version of the single pedestal secretary used in the Little House (0009) at the same time. One is designed with several swinging mirrors and was thought to be Mrs Dana's, and the other was fitted with cabinets containing drawers, for Mr Dana's folded shirts.

Master Bedroom
OPPOSITE: Wright's designs for beds were usually very simple. Two thick slabs of quarter-sawn oak make up the head- and foot-boards. Other beds in the house are of different sizes and proportions but retain the simplicity.

Living Room and Group of Chairs
ABOVE: This very high-ceilinged room which is not as breathtaking as the dining room or the studio does not get much attention, probably because there are no photographs of it before Mrs Dana's death in the 1940s. The art glass at the east windows is among the best of the house, and of Wright's career.

The chairs are uniformly lined up in a row, showing the fronts and the backs of an example of nearly every design found in the Dana House. They reflect amazing diversity and seeing these as a group reinforces the theory that the furniture was designed over several years, as the client discovered and the architect responded to new requirements.

Tall Back Spindle Dining Chair

OPPOSITE, ABOVE: This tall back dining chair is the finest and most balanced of Wright's career. There is restraint shown in the single trim strip at the seat rails. The tapers on the front legs and rear styles add considerable elegance, whilst the flare of the back leg adds a sense of stability. The top rail is broad but in proportion to the width of the back.

Medium Back Spindle Dining Chair

OPPOSITE, BELOW: Changing the proportion of the rail was important in order to maintain the balance between the height and the width.

Octagonal-backed Chair

ABOVE: Wright was always experimenting with different designs. This octagonal-back chair has a leg at each corner. There is a near-twin designed for the Littles of Peoria at the same time. The Little example has only four legs. The two legs at the rear are missing allowing the angled portion to cantilever.

Tall Back Spindle Dining Armchair
OPPOSITE, ABOVE: Unlike the Willits House example (0208), the Dana chair has spindles on the sides and the back. This adds considerable weight to the chair physically and visually.

Reclining Chair
OPPOSITE, BELOW LEFT: The basis of this chair is the spindle box chair as seen in the drawings from the Spencer article (June 1900) of the living room interior of the Heller House (9606), and from the second phase of furniture of Wright's Studio (9506). The cushions have been removed to expose the adjustable frames.

Slatted Armchair
OPPOSITE, BELOW RIGHT: This type of chair, which is a development of an upholstered chair, is occasionally referred to as an easy chair.

Settle
ABOVE: The trim wrapping the bottom of the legs reflects the detailing that was used throughout the Dana House. This settle has spindles on the sides and a lower back than those at the nearby fireplace.

Spindle Box Chair
OPPOSITE, ABOVE: This is inspired by the reclining chair for the Dana House and is a higher-backed development of the spindle box chair for Wright's studio. This unit has a wider back rail.

Entrance Chair
OPPOSITE, BELOW LEFT: Wright's sensitivity to design versus comfort is evident in pieces such as this one.

Slant-backed Box Armchair
OPPOSITE, BELOW RIGHT: One of the most unusual chairs, it seems out of place with the other designs. The slant back is out of proportion to the body of the chair and seems to be a spare part from another piece rather than designed for this particular one.

Square Table with Cabinet
ABOVE: Each of the four storage sections has access from two sides. The legs are not flared at the bottom. This table may have been designed for the library and like the library table, the edges are inset with quarter-inch borders.

Square Dining Table

OPPOSITE, ABOVE: The best proportioned of all of the square-leg dining tables, the Dana example shows considerable restraint. The four bands at the base of the legs are composed of two sets of trim, each of a different thickness. The single trim band at the bottom of the apron is sufficient on its own. The table is lower than most, of twenty-eight inches overall, while the two-and-a quarter inch thickness of the top is necessary to carry, and balance proportionally, the fifty-four inch square surface. The quarter-sawn oak top is waterfalled over the short edge and mitred on the longitudinal side. The flare at the base intensifies the illusion of mass and weight.

Long Dining Table

OPPOSITE, BELOW: Few dining rooms of Wright's Prairie period were large enough to accommodate a table as big as this. The multiple one-foot-wide extensions which can be added to the ends can make it up to twelve feet longer. It has been said that with the table set at maximum capacity it could accommodate up to forty people comfortably.

Print Table

ABOVE: Each of the print tables in all of the known examples have identical dimensions even though they were constructed at different times and occasionally of different woods. There is no evidence as to the maker. The two examples at the Dana House are both in quarter-sawn oak. The height of the table top is lower than most tables and when set in the centre of the room (as this unit often was) it is unclear what activity took place on it.

ART GLASS

This house not only contains the largest collection of art glass designs by Wright but also boasts the most elaborate and by far the best individual and innovative group designs. The stiff rolled colonial came which Wright used in the Dana House was still a new item on the market, available initially in Chicago only. The extra wide versions of this shape resulted in a half-inch-wide double crown style that was used in the Dana House windows.

The Dana designs are thematic, changing throughout the house. Even though each plane has a different motif, they are all linked by a common colour palette and principle of design.

The use of iridescent glass adds considerable interest to the designs and the quality of work. Linden Glass manufactured all the glass for the Dana House, advertising its commission in several architectural publications. However, in the advertisement which showed the fountain doors, a single door was portrayed in reverse, for the company neglected to realise that two different, not identical, doors were designed to make a pair. Hence, the advertisement failed to draw on the essence of the fountain doors – the organic quality. Initially, the similarities are stronger than the differences, but close examination reveals the differences; for example, no two leaves on one tree are the same, only the underlying framework remains consistent.

Wright's art glass was not limited to two-dimensional works. The first of his three-dimensional designs was for the Dana House in the form of the butterfly dining fixtures and three glass table lamps.

There is an extensive amount of glass in the Dana House: in soffits, under balconies, hanging in front of windows, pushing up from the basement and in every door and window. Extra sets of windows were introduced simply to hold more glass; for example, at the fountain.

The opportunity provided by Susan Lawrence Dana to realise the full potential of art glass windows was appreciated by Wright who took advantage of the situation and produced a total and unsurpassed work of art. The Dana House windows are now unfortunately protected by outer windows of bronze glass which obscure the beauty of the original art glass. The windows can no longer be seen in their stunning condition, but they will survive for many years to come.

Dana House entrance with the storm windows which were installed by Mr Thomas

Entry Fanlight

This is one of the few Wright houses with such a direct entrance. To further emphasise the entry door, Wright designed this magnificent fanlight. Even more unique is the butterfly motif, the only abstract design other than a plant form at this time. Colonial came adds the third dimension and iridescent silver glass enriches the fanlight. The glass appears to be blue-green in reflected light and straw-amber on the opposite side.

Entry Windows

ABOVE LEFT AND BELOW: The original design drawing is remarkably like the constructed window. The windows have a minimum amount of caming, hence allowing more light to enter the building. Milk glass and colonial came with accents of iridescent green glass are all used in these windows.

Gallery Window

ABOVE RIGHT: This window, on the east wall of the gallery, is a variation on the design of the entry glass. It is subtly altered to relate to, rather than replicate the pattern.

Entry Barrel Vault

OPPOSITE: The barrel vault seems to be in tension, pulled and held in place by the fanlights on either side. All three make up the composition.

Double Pedestal Lamp

ABOVE LEFT: The masterpiece of all of Wright's table lamps is this example from the Dana House. The design of the shade is a reflection of the sumac that is seen in many examples throughout the house. The side panels use the fumed and olive-green glass found in many of the windows. The cast bronze base has a patina on it reminiscent in many ways of the patina evident on Tiffany lamps. The iridescent glass panel set between the two uprights in the base is actually suspended from hinges at the crossbar which allows the glass panels to move. The panels of all of the art glass lamps are made this way. None is cracked and they remain in good condition.

Entry Ceiling Light

ABOVE RIGHT: This hanging ceiling light appears on the first-floor landing of the Dana House. The use of the inverted pyramid fleetingly resembles the similar one at the Barton House (0301). It incorporates a sumac flower motif at the centre with a protruding fin at each hip. The orange, red and yellow are the colours of the sumac in autumn.

Entry Single Pedestal Lamp

BELOW LEFT: Of all Wright's houses, the Dana House has the greatest number of freestanding lamps, with at least six still resident in the house. There were two of three patterns: two with single pedestals and one with a double pedestal. The ones at the Heath (0507) and Robie (0908) Houses are the only other documented examples.

Entry Floor Light

BELOW RIGHT: This light is unusually located over an opening to the basement. It is one of two sets of symmetrical lights just behind the Flower in the Crannied Wall sculpture at the entry, admitting light to the basement below and accenting the space from the reception/dining room level above. The lights are part of a wood frame that spans a vertical shaft of space which rises from the basement through the reception hall and reaches the roof. The pyramidal shape adds a third dimension to the otherwise flat structure. Neither before nor after did Wright design anything in the same vein.

Fountain Doors

OPPOSITE, ABOVE AND OVERLEAF: The fountain doors, as a pair, are the single most brilliant art glass designs ever conceived by Wright. They are similar and yet not symmetrical. The motif is one based on the wisteria vine as were some of the D D Martin House (0405) patterns. The entire line consists of six doors and four windows. There is a broad band of transparent milk glass that runs through the top of all of the individual units which is only noticeable in certain lighting conditions. The entire pattern appears to be woven into a base framework identical to the W E Martin House (0304). The full range of possibilities of the came variations is explored with thin single-crown and double-crown caming. These cames are known to have been manufactured by the Chicago Metallic Corporation which is still in business and in some cases continues to use the original dyes. Chicago Metallic is now more well known for its suspended ceiling T's than came manufacturing. The doors and windows of the Dana House were manufactured by the Linden Glass Company of Chicago and were proudly presented in one of its few pictorial advertisements (overleaf, above left). These designs have not had the notoriety of the Martin House 'tree of life' window, probably because they have remained with the building and not travelled the world on loan.

THE ARCHITECTURAL RECORD.
DESIGNED FOR DANA RESIDENCE
BY FRANK LLOYD WRIGHT ARCH.
MADE BY THE LINDEN GLASS CO.
LINDEN GLASS COMPANY
1216 MICHIGAN AV. CHICAGO : DESIGNERS · MANUFACTURERS
IMPORTERS : DECORATIVE LEADED GLASS · MEMORIAL
WINDOWS · GLASS MOSAIC · LAMPS · ELECTRIC FIXTURES
HAND EMBROIDERY · FURNITURE · DRAPERIES · RUGS
DECORATION & EVERYTHING FOR COMPLETE FURNISHING

Dining Room, Hanging Light
ABOVE LEFT: The State of Illinois purchased the Dana House from Thomas Publishing Co for less than the value of the four hanging lamps in the dining room. The State acquired the house and the rest of the furnishings for free. In the case of these hanging or butterfly lamps the shape of the lamp is again quite simple with two planes of vertical glass crossing in the middle. Between them span triangular sections and below these four others slant the other way. An illusionistic effect is produced, mainly by the angles of the squares and lines in the larger or upper triangles. They appear to be bent upwards towards the vertical planes. By mixing both clear and cathedral glass, the result is even more mysterious. The double-crown came is used effectively here.

Dining Room Soffit
ABOVE RIGHT: Similar but not identical to the soffit light at the entry fireplace, this is one of the lights under and behind the beautiful murals in the long walls of the dining room. These are often overlooked because of the overwhelming drama of other impressive appointments.

Dining Room Bay
This bay is often referred to as the breakfast end of the dining room. According to the oral histories conducted by the volunteers of the Dana-Thomas House, Mrs Dana ate breakfast here. The motif repeated in each of the casement windows is an abstract design of the Prairie sumac. Akin to the doors at the fountain, these patterns contain organic design irregularities, as close examination reveals.

Dining Room
OPPOSITE: The glass in the dining room is based on the sumac plant that grew wild in Illinois. The four hanging 'butterfly' lamps are the most abstract representation of this particular natural form, whilst the bay windows and the clerestory are the most representational. The colours of the sumac patterns in the clerestory are of deep orange, while the bay windows are light yellow. Curiously, the glass is the same but the light contrast alters the perception of the colour. The colour of the soffit lighting which runs the length of the barrel vault is a mixture of the two, but in higher contrast tones. The background glass is translucent, replacing the clear plate glass used in the windows.

Dining Room Lunette Window
ABOVE: Maintaining the dining room motif of the sumac, these windows are similar but do not repeat the designs in the bay below. Even the manner in which the ends of the branches are rendered differentiates the design from the breakfast bay examples. Without the brick apartment building, it must have been a wonderful view on a sunny summer morning or evening.

Master Bedroom Door
OPPOSITE: Nearly every plane in the Dana House contains a different art glass design. An abstract image of a plant is used again in this unusual pattern.

Master Bedroom Window
ABOVE: The east windows of the master bedroom are part of a larger composition which includes the east-facing windows in the living room. The scale of these patterns relates to the scale of the entire eastern facade rather than to the individual openings. In contrast to the white milk glass of the doors to the master bedroom, the east window glass is largely iridescent, similar to that used for the butterfly fanlights at the entrance.

Living Room Doors
OPPOSITE: The double-crown came does not carry through into the sidelights by the doors. This use of the wider came in this fashion does not appear to be as successful as in other designs. This is partly because the design lacks one particular focal point.

Living Room Window
ABOVE: These photographs illustrate the changes of appearance of the same pattern on the same day. The iridescent glass appears blue-green from the exterior and straw-amber from the interior, as exemplified by so many other art glass windows dating from this era. The white glass is much brighter from the outside than the inside. The success of both of these designs shows the skill Wright had gained in this particular media.

Gallery Stair Hanging Light
OVERLEAF: The fifth hanging butterfly light is not an exact duplicate of those in the dining room. There are refined differences, such as the base of the light which is the most obvious to the casual observer. The music cabinet is unique as it is the only freestanding piece of furniture to incorporate art glass in Wright's work. The cabinet at the base appears to be configured to hold sheet music. The function of the glassed area and the drawer remains a mystery. No logical theories or explanations seem to exist.

Fernery Doors

ABOVE LEFT: At one end of the long hall known as the fernery (because of the garden area), doors lead into the Gallery at the west end of the house. The doors were designed to give an impression of ferns, hence the delicate overall pattern which seems to cascade down the doors echoing the movement of the frond of a Boston fern.

Fernery Windows

ABOVE RIGHT: These windows are identical to those of the William E Martin House (0304) and are the basis of the fountain doors, making good use of double-crown came.

Library Door

BELOW LEFT: A design very close to the one at the Barton House (0301) is exemplified in the library door panel which leads into the backyard. The olive-green glass in the central chevrons occupies every third, rather than the usual alternate, opening.

Library Window

BELOW RIGHT: After seeing so many windows which used came in a variety of ways, this window is unexpectedly simple. The usual borders which appear at the top and base of Wright's windows are absent. The abstract design is once again based on a Prairie plant and the glass is of the same iridescent straw-amber colour as most of the glass in the house.

DECORATIVE ARTS

Frieze
ABOVE: The mouldmaker was located in the basement of the Dana House and new frieze panels were made on site to replace the originals which had loosened with time. This design is more Art Deco in style than one would expect for 1900-1902, the date of design. The pattern is more than two inches deep, making good use of the play of light and shadow. The original descriptions lead one to believe that the gypsum plaster was of the same colour as the brick-work, placing it in the same category as the other friezes.

Mural
OPPOSITE AND OVERLEAF: It is a near miracle that this delicate mural has survived, because the Dana House was virtually abandoned for fifteen years in the 1920s and 30s. The mural was rendered by George Niedecken, a young man from Milwaukee, and his signature can still be seen on it. The motif of the house is the sumac, which is shown in its full vibrant colour along with the goldenrod plant in the mural. This scene was quite a familiar one throughout the Midwest with sumac banks growing wild nearly everywhere. The effect of the colours changes dramatically when the natural northern light shines upon it.

Flower in the Crannied Wall
OPPOSITE, ABOVE: Gates Potteries and Richard Bock collaborated with Wright to design and produce this beautiful work. It is signed 'Teco', a mark of the Gates Potteries. There are photographs that show a block in the right hand side of the figure, but as yet no actual block has been found. Wright had one of these made for himself. It has not been seen in any of the Oak Park photographs, but it can be seen in the inner garden at Taliesin. It indicates that structures (presumably buildings would be included in this equation) and life, as represented by the human figure, stem from a common ancestry – mother earth, as Wright referred to it.

Fountain

BELOW AND OVERLEAF: Apparently the family depicted in the fountain is Wright's own, as rendered again by Richard Bock. It is interesting to note that the opening in the jar from where water flowed, is backlit by an electric light. This light made the water sparkle much like fibre optics today. This model, from Greenville College, the Bock Collection, is nearly identical to the finished work.

Exterior and Interior Drawings

ABOVE AND OVERLEAF: These two interiors and one exterior of the Dana House in Springfield illustrate what Wright had in mind before the final decision was made by the client. The renderings and presentation drawings were all controlled, the ideal solution by Wright.

Dining Room Mural

BELOW: The dining room mural has been over-cleaned and some of the vibrancy has been washed away but the colours inspired by Wright – the sumac and the goldenrod – still come through. The mural was painted by George Niedecken, who later became a decorator and worked with Wright on many commissions.

Mural – East Panel

Mural – West Panel

Mural – North Panel

Mural – North Panel. Detail

Mural – Detail

Mural – Detail without Lights, South Panel

Wall Sconces

Hundreds of these wall sconces can be found in the Dana House. Some of them were also configured for gas lighting since electricity was still new and occasionally unreliable. According to some correspondence of a draftsman in Wright's Oak Park office, these were designed by the head of the drafting room, Walter Burley Griffin, an 1899 graduate of the University of Illinois. Griffin later town-planned Canberra, and many buildings in Australia and the Midwest in the United States.

OAK RIDGE CEMETERY

Susan was buried in her family plot in Oak Ridge Cemetery, located at the north side of Springfield. These are the plots for the Maxey (Susan's mother) and Lawrence (Susan's father) families as well as her own. There are eighteen people listed on the four sides of the tall granite monument, dating from her great-grandparents who were born in 1791 and 1794, to two of her husbands and her two infant sons. The turn of the century was obviously very difficult for Susan, as she lost her first husband in 1899, her father in 1901, her grandmother in 1902 and her mother in 1905. It is interesting to note that two people were buried at the plot who were not family members: Susan's spiritualist and trance medium, Celia Hughes, and Mary Peek, a leader in the Unity Church of Practical Christianity.

Susan's third husband, Charles A Gehrmann, whom she divorced, is buried just north of Susan in his own family plot. He died on May 20, 1944 two years before Susan's death on February 20, 1946.

This cemetery is also the site of President Abraham Lincoln's tomb and memorial.

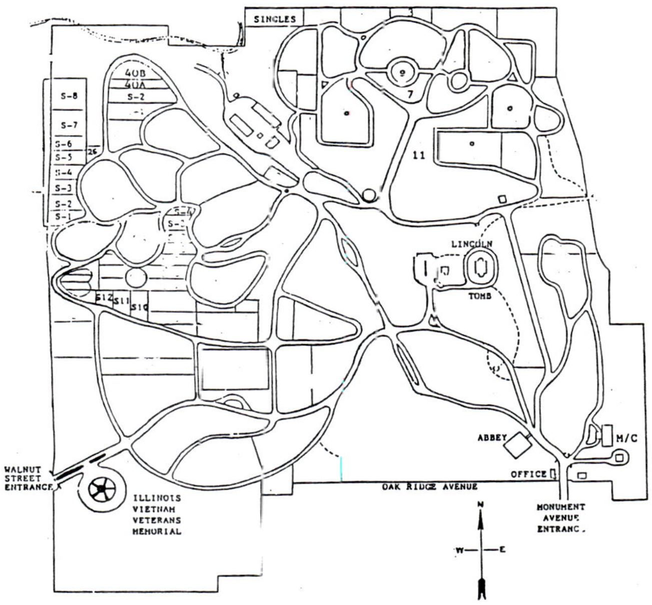

Burial Monument

The Monument is tall and made of granite. It notes eighteen names including Susan's parents, grandparents, two husbands and two children. Just over the road is the Lincoln Tomb. *Photo by Tom Stevens, Photo Resource Center, Springfield.*

Above: Oak Ridge Cemetery Plan

Number 11 is the site of the Lawrence marker. Number 7 is the Gehrmann lots and includes Susan's third husband. *Plan courtesy of Rich L Branom and Oak Ridge Cemetery.*

LAWRENCE MEMORIAL LIBRARY

Even Henry-Russell Hitchcock was mistaken as to what the Lawrence Memorial Library (0509) actually was. In his important book *In the Nature of Materials*, he listed it as: '1905 Lawrence Memorial Library interior for Mrs R D Lawrence, Springfield, Ill'. Grant Manson in his book, *The First Golden Age*, makes no mention of it. Many thought the Gallery, attached at the west end of the Dana House, was the Memorial Library, as Susan regularly loaned books to the local children. There was talk of a photograph showing it under construction after the main house was completed. The earliest photograph of the actual room entitled the school in which it was located, the Lincoln School. Much confusion and mystery surrounded this small and rather unimportant Wright design.

During the early years of the State of Illinois ownership of the Dana House several volunteers and State employees were hard at work researching every detail of the Dana House. Through diligence, they were able to determine the proper location and attribution of the Lawrence Memorial Library.

Mr Lawrence was the Mayor of Springfield for one term in 1890 after having been defeated in the previous election. He had been appointed to various commissions by two previous governors – Cullom and Tanner – as far back as 1877, had served on the Board of Education for eight years (1893-1901) and had been President of the same for six of those years.

Susan's commitment to education was further revealed by the two contests she proposed for the students of Springfield's schools. One was for an oratorical contest and the other for a manual training competition. First prize was a $20 gold piece and second prize, $10. Susan was interested in having a Lawrence Memorial Library of Wright's design included in the school to commemorate her father's interest in education.

A school constructed by the Springfield Board of Education was named after Rheuna Lawrence in 1903. It was not designed by Wright but by George Helme, a local Springfield architect, at a cost of $43,550 and was built by C W Black. Construction began in May 1903. It was noted in April 1906 that Mrs Dana was completing the library. Curiously, it was not until 1910 that the School Board thanked Susan for the library. This may have been because the library was not fully operational until that time due to the purchase and cataloguing of books.

An original drawing of the room is housed at the Archives of The Frank Lloyd Wright Foundation in Arizona. It is noted as: 'Lawrence Memorial Library/Springfield, Illinois', and dated 7 March 1905, a few months after the completion of the Dana House and the date on which Susan's mother died.

Examples of Wright-designed tables and chairs from the library are located at the Dana House. The Lawrence School is located several blocks to the southwest of the Dana House at 2nd and Laurel. The building is now known as the Lawrence Adult Education Center and the room has been rebuilt according to the original plans and photographs.

Information for the Library was gathered and originally written by Jaqueline Wright, Ed Russo, James Allen, John Patterson and Richard Taylor.

Lawrence Memorial Library, old photograph
The seated children may have been stage-managed for this photograph. The note indicates it is the Lincoln Library, and not the Lawrence Memorial Library, but in the Lawrence School. The work was removed but was recently reinstalled according to this photograph and the original drawings found at the Frank Lloyd Wright Archives in Scottsdale. *DH 89.F.8.90 from the Archives of the Dana-Thomas House, State Historic Site.*

Lawrence Memorial Library, new photograph
This is the new reconstruction of the Library, now an adult center. The tables, chairs and woodwork are all new. *Photo by Steve Ritchie, Photo Resource Center, Springfield.*

Lawrence Memorial Library Table and Chair
These have been at the Dana House for years and it has always been assumed that this is where they originated. No one guessed that they were from the Lawrence Memorial Library. The volunteers of the State Site discovered the library and the origin of these pieces.

BIBLIOGRAPHY

Introductory remarks concerning the Dana House

The Dana House was first published in the *American Architect & Building News*, 24 August 1907, as the 'House and Studio of Mrs Mary Lawrence, Springfield, Illinois'.

With her interest in photography, it is surprising that there are no photographs that have been identified as Susan Dana's. With such an elaborate project, it is also surprising that so few photographs of the early days of the interior and exterior of the Dana House have been located. Susan's personal papers must have been lost. Even the local newspaper in Springfield has very little in the form of photographic evidence.

The Dana House was included in the 1910 and the 1911 editions of the Wasmuth portfolio, in the form of drawings and in photographs. Both were nearly identical.

An archive containing 1,000 articles and documents, fifty historic photographs and many restoration photographs exists at the Dana-Thomas House site and is available to scholars for review and study.

Bibliography

American Architect & Building News, 24 August 1907, 'House and Studio of Mrs Mary Lawrence, Springfield, Illinois'.

Architectural Record, May 1908. Certain editions of the magazine included advertisements for Linden Glass and John Ayers. They showed the fountain doors of Linden Glass manufacture and some Wright-designed furniture built by Ayers.

Appraisement Bill, Estate of Susan Z Lawrence, Incompetent, Filed 17 December 1942, Probate Court. This is a typed, single spaced forty-seven page document with an extremely detailed inventory of all Susan's possessions and the value of each. There are several items of note. Locations of possessions are noted, including a safe deposit vault, the Dana House and the White Cottage. Much of it is filled with lists of fabric and clothing. All books are noted individually. The forty dining room chairs and sixteen low back studio chairs (probably from the Dana Memorial Library) were listed and valued at $0.25 each. The most highly valued item was a Van Briggle at $45.00. Everything from carriages to buttons, along with coins, paper money, china, crystal, jewellery and several guns were included. In total, all Susan's possessions were valued at $57,386.11.

Allen, James R, 'Springfield's Dana-Thomas House', *Historic Illinois*, Volume 4, No 3, October 1981, pp1-3, 12-14. This is the first article about the State of Illinois' purchase of the Dana House. It gives a short but revealing history of the house.

Allen, James R, Hallmark, Donald P, Taylor, Richard S, *Dana-Thomas House*, 1989, Dana-Thomas House Foundation, 18 page paperback. All eras are covered, some in colour, but mostly in black and white photos.

Allen, James, Patterson, John, Taylor, Richard, 'Frank Lloyd Wright and Springfield's Lawrence School', *Historic Illinois*, April 1982, pp1-3, 12-13. At last someone has solved the mystery of the Lawrence Memorial Library and confirmed that it is not in, or part of, the Dana House. Located in nearby Lawrence School, the library was designed by Wright in 1905.

American Architect and Building News, 24 August 1907, 'The House and Studio of Mrs Mary Lawrence, Springfield, Illinois', plate only. It is unusual that it was not noted as the Dana House.

Bock, Richard W, *Memoirs of an American Artist*, C C Publishing Co, Los Angeles, 1989. This is Bock's autobiography, containing information on Susan Lawrence and the Dana House. It was assembled by his daughter Dorthea Bock Pierre.

Brooks, H Allen (ed), *Writings on Wright: Selected Commentary on Frank Lloyd Wright*, MIT Press, Cambridge, 1981, 229 pages, 45 illustrations. Two photographs are of note: a detail of the frieze of the Winslow House and the interior of the Hanna House.

Cavanaugh, Tom R and Thomas, Payne E L, *Bannerstone House*, Charles C Thomas Publishers, Springfield, Illinois, 1970, 41 pages. Written and published by the people who owned and occupied the house for nearly forty years, this history of the Dana House contains some unique new and contemporary photographs of decorative details. The book was well researched and contains information based on several interviews and even lengthy correspondence with Wright.

Chicago Tribune, 15 August 1981, Section 1, p3, 'Wright House in Springfield Saved', Paul Gapp. This illustrated article discusses the Dana House sale by Thomas Publishing to the State of Illinois, with a short accurate history.

Clark, Robert Judson (ed), *The Arts and Crafts Movement in America 1876-1916*, Princeton University Press, Princeton, 1972, 192 pages, 295 illustrations. This book includes graphics, furniture, metal and pottery.

Dana-Thomas House Staff, *Dana-Thomas House Volunteer Manual*, Historic Preservation Agency, Springfield, Illinois, 1990. This manual is used as a reference for the volunteer tour guides.

Darling, Sharon S, *Chicago Ceramics & Glass: An Illustrated History from 1871 to 1933*, Chicago Historical Society, Chicago, 1979, 221 pages, 221 illustrations. This book covers Wright's contributions with a Dana House lamp and dining room window, and includes a considerable amount of very good information about Chicago's ceramic and glass makers.

Darling, Sharon S, *Chicago Furniture: Art, Craft & Industry from 1833 to 1983*, Chicago Historical Society (W W Norton, New York), Chicago, 1984, 416 pages, 340 illustrations. Contains a good section on John Ayers who is associated with at least some of the Dana furniture.

Darling, Sharon S, *Teco: Pottery of the Prairie School*, Erie Museum of Art, Erie, Pennsylvania, 1989. The book shows one of the rare Teco jardinieres (umbrella stands) that Wright designed for the Dana House. At least two of them were cast.

Diederich, David, *The Dana-Thomas House, Fact Book & Tour Guide*, 1992, 72 pages, paperback. Good source for very detailed information about the site, the house and its history, and all those involved in the house over its history.

Diederich, David, *Susan Lawrence Dana: An Anthology*. Unpublished manuscript concerning letters, newspaper articles, and other written information about Susan and her house.

Drexler, Arthur, *Drawings of Frank Lloyd Wright*, Horizon Press, New York, 1962, 303 plates. Twenty-four plates deal with furniture, glass and decorative art. Plates 11 & 12 include preliminary drawings of the Wright's studio and the Dana House entry hall.

Elliott, Scott, *Frank Lloyd Wright*, Kelmscott Gallery, Chicago, 1981, 64 pages, black and white catalogue. One of the original Linden Art Glass Co. advertisements featuring the Dana fountain doors, as well as a Wasmuth plate.

de Fries, H (ed), *Frank Lloyd Wright: Aus dem Lebenswerke eines Architekten*, Mit Uber 100 Abbildungen und 9 Farbensafeln, Berlin Verlag Ernst Pollak, 1926, 80 pages, mainly black and white pictures.

Futagawa, Yukio (ed/photographer), *Houses of Frank Lloyd Wright I*, ADA Edita, Tokyo, 1975, 184 pages. This book contains many familiar, as well as obscure, interiors and details of the first forty-five years of Wright's practice, pre-Usonian.

Haight, Deborah S and Blume, Peter F, *Frank Lloyd Wright: The Library from the Francis W Little House*, Allentown Art Museum, Allentown, Pennsylvania, 1978, 20 pages. A very nice little booklet containing good photographs of the art glass window designs.

Hallmark, Donald P, 'Frank Lloyd Wright's Dana-Thomas House: Its History, Acquisition and Preservation', *Illinois Historical Journal*, Summer 1989, (Vol 82, No 2), Revised 1992, 14 pages, paperback. All black and white photographs, with a good history of the house and the two principal participants.

Hallmark, Donald P, 'Richard W. Bock, Sculptor. Part I: The Early Work', *The Prairie School Review*, Vol 8, No 1, First Quarter, 1971, pp5-18. This article examines Bock's work from Sullivan to the first few years of this century.

Hallmark, Donald P, 'Richard W Bock, Sculptor. Part II: The Mature Collaborations', *The Prairie School Review*, Vol 8, No 2, Second Quarter, 1971, pp5-29. In 1897, Wright and Bock collaborated for the first time on the Heller, Dana and D D Martin Houses, the Larkin building and Midway Gardens. All are well illustrated.

Hanks, David A, *The Decorative Designs of Frank Lloyd Wright*, E P Dutton, New York, 1979, 232 pages. The first book which covers Wright's non-architectural work. There are very good sections on the history of the pieces and their makers. Some of the drawings of the Dana House art glass are shown.

Hanks, David A, *Frank Lloyd Wright: Preserving an Architectural Heritage, Decorative Designs from The Domino's Pizza Collection*, E P Dutton, New York, 1989, 156 pages. All objects in the collection are in colour, including a piece of the original painted frieze and one of the copper urns.

Heinz, Thomas A, 'Frank Lloyd Wright's Art Glass: A Photo Essay', *Frank Lloyd Wright Newsletter*, Vol 4, No 1, 1st Quarter, 1981, pp6-19. Thirty-nine photographs of Wright windows appear in black and white.

Heinz, Thomas A, *Architectural Monographs 18: Frank Lloyd Wright*, Academy Editions, London, 1992, 144 pages. Contains eleven colour photographs of the Dana House, showing the house without the plaster frieze and before State ownership.

Heinz, Thomas A, *Frank Lloyd Wright*, Academy Editions, London, 1982. This book was one of the earliest all-colour books on Wright. There are several photographs of the Dana House.

Heinz, Thomas A, *Frank Lloyd Wright: Glass Art*, Academy Editions, London, 1994. Pages 37 to 61 are reprinted in the Dana House book. The first comprehensive look at the subject includes most known glass designs with several helpful appendices. Sections on sculpture, dinnerware and low relief designs are discussed.

Heinz, Thomas A, *Frank Lloyd Wright: Interiors and Furniture*, Academy Editions, London 1994. Pages 31 to 47 are reprinted in the Dana House book. The first comprehensive look at the furniture its context, and how they related to one another. Sections on colour, fabrics and rugs are included.

Heinz, Thomas A, *Frank Lloyd Wright: Stained Glass*, Gibbs Smith Publisher, Salt Lake City, 1994. Nine colour photographs of the Dana House are published with many close-up details of other buildings included.

Heinz, Thomas A. *Frank Lloyd Wright: Furniture*, Gibbs Smith Publisher, Salt Lake City, Utah, 1994. The dining set, music cabinet and a chair from the Dana Memorial Library in the Lawrence School (not Lincoln as noted) are shown in colour.

Heinz, Thomas A. *Frank Lloyd Wright: Midwest*, Gibbs Smith Publisher, Salt Lake City, Utah, 1994. Five photographs of the Dana House are included, along with a stunning photo of the Flower-in-the-Crannied-Wall sculpture.

Heinz, Thomas A. 'Frank Lloyd Wright: Dana House 1903', *Architectural Design*, London, No 1-2, 1980, pp68-71. A short note about the Dana House, its condition, state of preservation, and the extensive holdings of furniture and art glass.

Heinz, Thomas A. 'Dana House is Sold to the State of Illinois', *Frank Lloyd Wright Newsletter*, Vol 4, No 3, Third Quarter, 1981, p47. There is a good shot of the hanging art glass lights in the ballroom of the Dana House.

Hitchcock, Henry-Russell, *Frank Lloyd Wright*, Cahiers d'Art, Paris, 1928, 37 pages. A short book on Wright's work between 1902 and 1923, including the Dana House.

Hitchcock, Henry-Russell, *In the Nature of Materials*, Duell Sloan & Pierce, New York, 1942, 141 pages. Still the best single volume on Wright's work. There are three Henry Fruerman photographs, the originals of which have not been located, showing the exterior and interior in their early forms. The house is dealt with in a single paragraph. Hitchcock's dating of the buildings is one of the most accurate.

Illinois State Journal. A set of four newspaper articles relating directly to our knowledge of the Dana House was published on 17 December 1904; 23 December 1904; 30 June 1941; and 1 July 1943. These are noted in the Cavanaugh booklet.

Inland Architect, Volume 25, Number 4, May 1981, pp2, 46-47, 'Mrs Dana's Place'. The house, its importance, possible future use and potential sale is discussed, with seven photographs.

Kaufmann, Edgar, Jr, *Drawings for a Living Architecture*, Horizon Press, New York, 1959. Five black and white drawings are reproduced of the main hall, gallery, entrance archway with gate (the copper gate has been removed but can be seen in early photographs), fanlight over front door, and the design for the fountain window.

Lipman, Jonathan, *Frank Lloyd Wright Retrospective*, Tokyo, 1991. This book covers the Dana House with three photographs and a Wasmuth drawing. The text is in Japanese with some notes in English.

Manson, Grant Carpenter, *Frank Lloyd Wright to 1910: The First Golden Age*, Van Nostrand Reinhold Company, New York, 1958, 228 pages, 135 illustrations An excellent source for early interiors not found elsewhere. The Dana House is illustrated and discussed in eight pages, and includes the earliest view of the foundations rising around the Lawrence's Italianate villa.

Meehan, Patrick J, *Frank Lloyd Wright: A Research Guide to Archival Sources*, Garland Publishing Inc, New York, 714 pages, 115 illustrations. This book is useful in many different ways. The listings of the holding of each archive also contains a listing of the objects and the papers.

Peisch, Mark L, *The Chicago School of Architecture*, Random House, New York, 1964, 178 pages, 42 illustrations. An early and scarce work on Wright, Walter Burley Griffin and others.

Riley, Terence, et al, *Frank Lloyd Wright, Architect*, Museum of Modern Art, New York, 1994, 344 pages. This book includes several photographs and drawings of the Dana House, including an excellent colour reproduction of the drawing of the dining room.

Rubin, Susan Goldman, *Frank Lloyd Wright*, Harry Abrams, New York, 1994, 92 pages. A children's book about Wright's life and work includes a short piece on the Dana House, including two photographs.

Russell, Frank (ed), *A Century of Chair Design*, Academy Editions, London, 1980, 160 pages, 350 illustrations. Wright is covered in eight pieces, some in colour, including the interior of his Oak Park dining room, Evans arm chair, Hanna dining chair and a Little House side chair.

Russell, Frank (ed), *Art Nouveau Architecture*, Academy Editions, London, 1979, 332 pages. A chapter on Frank Lloyd Wright is included, containing photographs of the stairway window of the Heller House and an interior of the Dana House in colour.

Spencer, Brian A (ed), *The Prairie School Tradition*, Whitney Library of Design, New York, 1979, 304 pages. This volume contains a large section on Wright. Many of the drawings are familiar but there are some more rare ones, including the Luxfer prism tile, tall copper weed holder, Coonley House rug patterns, Oscar Steffens and Lake Geneva Inn windows, and Sondern chairs.

Sprague, Paul E, *The Drawings of Louis Henry Sullivan*, Princeton University Press, Princeton, New Jersey, 1979. This is a catalogue of the Frank Lloyd Wright Collection at the Avery Library, Columbia University, New York. It contains several drawings that may have been worked on by Wright. It is very well written in its commentaries and notes.

Sprague, Paul E, 'Wright's Dana House', *Outdoor Illinois*, Vol 12, No 8, October 1973, pp12-18. Fine photographs accompany this article. A master bedroom cabinet is illustrated.

The State Journal-Register, 28 November 1965, 'The Woman Who Lived in a Fabulous Home'. A short note about Susan Dana.

The State Journal-Register, 24 January 1981, p1, 'Dana Home being put up for Sale', Dan Cronin. An illustrated note about the sale of the Dana House.

The State Journal-Register, 21 March 1981, p1, 'Wright's Granddaughter takes tour of Dana House', Dana Cvetan. An illustrated article about a visit by Elizabeth Wright Ingraham.

Sweeney, Robert L, *Frank Lloyd Wright: An Annotated Bibliography*, Hennessey & Ingalls, Inc, Los Angeles, 1978, 303 pages, 12 plates. This excellent bibliography also contains a short illustrated history of Wright graphics from the Eve of St Agnes, 1896, to the first Taliesin Square Paper of 1940. It ends with the last entry of 1976. One wishes Mr Sweeney would publish the addendum soon.

Taylor, Richard S, 'New Thought in the Twenties: The Case of Springfield Illinois', *The Historian*, 49 (1987) pp329-347.

Taylor, Richard S, *Susan Lawrence*. Unpublished manuscript in the collection of the State Historical Library, a division of the Illinois Historic Preservation Agency, Springfield, Illinois. A thorough account of the life of Susan Lawrence.

Van Rensselaer, Marina Griswold, *Henry Hobson Richardson and His Works*, Dover Publications, New York, 1969, 154 pages, 97 illustrations. A very good overview of Richardson's work. It shows many of the ideas and architectural solutions that were undertaken and redefined by Wright. Chapter 19 is particulary revealing as it describes Taliesin and the Oak Park studio very well.

Wallace, Joseph, *Past and Present of Sangamon County Illinois*, S J Clarke Publishing Co, Chicago, 1904. A general history of the county and the people who shaped it, including Rheuna Lawrence.

Wright, Frank Lloyd, *An Autobiography*, Longmans, Green and Co, New York, 1932, 372 pages, illustrated. This edition had both photographs and graphics at the front of each chapter in black, white and red. The 1942 edition had some of the same graphics with silver and red ink on brown. These are some of the best of Wright's abstractions, particularly the one of Taliesin introducing Book Four. There are no photographs of the Dana House.

Wright Frank Lloyd, *Ausgefuhrte Bauten und Entwurfe von Frank LLoyd Wright* (Studies and Executed Buildings of Frank Lloyd Wright) 100 lithographs, E Wasmuth, Berlin, 1910. The Dana House entry reads: 'Plate XXXI, General view of a city dwelling for Mrs Susan L Dana, Springfield, Illinois, 1899 [sic]. A home designed to accommodate the art collection of its owner and for entertaining extensively, somewhat elaborately worked out in detail. Fixtures and furnishings designed with the furniture. It is not entirely new. The old house, which was incorporated in the structure, is outlined by a heavy line on the plan. The gallery is designed as a gathering place for the artistic activities of the community, and to accommodate the collection made by its owner. It is connected by a covered passage with the house, the passage itself serving as a conservatory. The dining room and gallery extend through two stories, with the ceiling formed in the roof. The terracotta figure at the entrance was modelled by Richard W Bock, sculptor. The interior walls are of cream-coloured brick, closely laid. The woodwork is of freely marked red oak. The sand-finished plaster ceilings are ribbed with wood and stained. Around the dining-room is a decoration of sumac (the plant motif for the decoration of the house proper) and fall flowers stained in the sand-finished background by George Niedecken. The furniture and fittings were designed with the buildings. Many of the drawings of the buildings are not precisely as they were constructed. Wright took liberties in interpreting what he wanted people to see in his buildings versus being historically accurate. Some of the drawings are based on tracings of the photographs'.

Wright Frank Lloyd, *Ausgefuhrte Bauten*, E Wasmuth, Berlin, 1911. This was published a year after the double elephant portfolio with photographs of many of the executed buildings in the drawings. It is largely a republication of the March 1908 *Architectural Record* article.

Wright, Frank Lloyd, *The Early Work*, Horizon Press, New York, 1968, 143 pages. An updated and reformatted republishing of the 1911 Wasmuth book, this edition makes some additions and deletions to the original. It is one of the best to show the early interiors, such as Browne's Bookstore, Coonley House, Robie House, Dana House, Bradley House and the D D Martin House. One only wishes that there were more of these rare views.

Wright, Frank Lloyd, 'In the Cause of Architecture', *Architectural Record*, March 1908, pp155-221. An essay with fifty-six pages of photographs, including the Gallery, dining room with the original Teco pottery and the draperies of the Dana House. In the accompanying text, the house is referred to as the Lawrence House and is stylistically grouped along with the Bradley, Hickox and Davenport Houses. The common thread is the gabbled roofs.

Wright, Frank Lloyd, 'In the Cause of Architecture – Glass', *Architectural Record*, July 1928, pp10-16. This article includes a photograph of one of the windows from the Dana House as exhibited in the Chicago Art Institute show. The date for the house is noted as 1899.

Wright, Frank Lloyd, *Monograph Volume 1: 1887-1901*. A D A Edita, Tokyo, 1985, edited and photographed by Yukio Futagawa, text by Bruce Brooks Pfeiffer. There are some photographs and four drawings are illustrated. Two are floorplans of the first and second floor and the others are elevations and sections in colour. These give more of a sense of the verticality of the spaces and are worth studying.

Wright, Frank Lloyd, *Selected Houses: 1*. A D A Edita, Tokyo, pp78-107. All the photographs shown were taken after the recent work was completed.

Of further note, there are fourteen drawings of glass, one of sculpture, but none of furniture in the Frank Lloyd Archives, Taliesin West, Scottsdale, Arizona.

INDEX

Dana House Statistics

Excavations and Foundations began: July 1902
Drawings revised: January 1903
Completed: October 1904

Cost: probable $45,000 for construction and $15,000 for furnishings and fixtures

Size: 12,600 square feet
35 rooms
6 bedrooms, 5 bathrooms
6 fireplaces
3 main levels, 16 levels in all

The house is now known as the Dana-Thomas House Historic Site, Historic Preservation Agency, State of Illinois.

Address: 301 East Lawrence Avenue
Springfield
Illinois 62703
USA